'BIKE BIOGRAPHY

This page enables you to compile a list of useful data on your motorcycle, so that whenever you're ordering spares or just checking the tyre pressures, all the key information - the information that is 'personal' to your motorcycle - is within easy reach.

Registration number:..

Make and Model:...

Colour:...

Date of first registration: ....

Date of manufacture (if different): ....

Frame number:..

Engine number:...

Gearbox number:...

Tyre size

    Front: ....Rear:................................

Tyre pressure (ridden solo)

    Front: ....Rear:................................

Tyre pressure (with pillion passenger)

    Front: ....Rear:................................

Insurance

    Name, address and telephone number of insurer: ....

    ....

    Expiry date: ....

    MOT test due: ....

Modifications

    Information that might be useful when you need to purchase parts:...

    ....

    ....

Suppliers

    Address and telephone number of your dealer and parts supplier: ....

    ....

A PORTER PUBLISHING BOOK

First published 1995

Published and Produced by
Porter Publishing
The Storehouse
Little Hereford Street
Bromyard
Hereford HR7 4DE
England

British Library Cataloguing in Publication Data

A catalogue record for this book is available from the British Library.

ISBN 1-899238-08-5

Series Editor: Lindsay Porter
Design: Lindsay Porter and Lyndsay Berryman, Pineapple Publishing
Printed in England by The Trinity Press, Worcester

Other Titles in this Series

Absolute Beginners Service Guide
Caravan Owner's Manual and Service Guide
Diesel Car Engine Service Guide
Land Rover Defender, 90 & 110 Service Guide
Land Rover Series I, II, III Service Guide
MGB (including MGC, MGB GT V8) Service Guide
MG Midget and Austin Healey Sprite Service Guide
Mini (all models 1959-on) Service Guide
VW Beetle (all models to 1980) Service Guide

- With more titles in production -

Classic 'Bike

Step-by-Step Service Guide

by Jeff Clew

FOREWORD

Ihave known the author, Jeff Clew, for many years, as a result of both his writings in a plethora of magazines and books, as well as his involvement with the Vintage Motor Cycle Club. His reputation as a technical author has been built over a long time and is further enhanced by the format and content of this excellent and well-designed book.

I feel sure that those who have just acquired their first old bike and are starting out their courtship, will find their path of true love with the machinery smoothed by ownership of the "Classic Bike Step-by-Step Service Guide". If Jeff's book is kept in the workshop, near the toolbox, it will be an asset referred to constantly and, I hope, will allow the love affair with old motorcycles to develop into a full-scale romance.

Robin James
Leominster
1995

CONTENTS

Introduction

Over the years I have owned over sixty different motorcycles, ranging from a 1914 550cc Triumph to a 1957 192cc Velocette Valiant. Only two of them have been new, one bought by my father. Whether out of compassion or anguish I shall never know, for he must have suffered many a rude awakening in the small hours of the morning, disturbed by the sound of his eldest son pushing a defunct motorcycle up the steeply sloping front path before collapsing in near exhaustion once it was safely inside the garage. I learnt my lessons the hard way, knowing that any motorcycle is only enjoyable to own if it's reliable, safe and basically sound - and the only way of being sure it stays that way is to service it regularly. That's why Porter Publishing has set about creating a series of Service Guides for cars and motorcycles which aim to provide you, the owner, with all the information you will need to keep your vehicle in tip-top condition. If your classic bike is not yet as reliable as it might be, you will be able to give it a 'super service', using the information found in the Servicing Section of this book, and bring it back into good, reliable order.

Having joined the Haynes Publishing Group in late 1972 to originate their range of Motorcycle Owners Workshop Manuals, I hope much of what I have learnt along the way is reflected in this step-by-step service guide. In this respect I would like to thank Lindsay Porter for giving me this opportunity to originate this first in a new series of service guides, based on first-hand practical experience.

Porter Publishing Service Guides are the first books to give all the service information you will need, with step-by-step instructions, along with a complete Service History section for you to complete and fill in as you carry our regular maintenance on your machine over the months ahead. Using the information contained in this book, you will be able to:

◆ see for yourself how to carry out every Service task, from weekly and monthly checks, right up to the longer-term maintenance items.

◆ carry out regular safety checks, saving a fortune by discovering and eliminating faults that are in their early stages of development, over the years to come.

◆ enhance the value of your classic bike by having available a full Service History of every maintenance task you have carried out.

We hope you will enjoy keeping your classic motorcycle in first class trim while saving lots of money by servicing it yourself with the help of this book. Happy motorcycling!

Acknowledgements

A great deal of effort goes into any book, especially one such as this which covers something like 25 years of British motorcycle manufacture and every conceivable make and model. In this respect I am eternally grateful to the many friends and acquaintances I contacted, all of whom responded to my many questions and offered advice so very willingly. All showed enthusiasm for this very ambitious project, to which I was already giving a great deal of thought at the time when I retired from the Haynes Publishing Group.

I am especially grateful to NGK Spark Plugs (UK) Limited who provided information about sparking plug conditions and gave permission to use their photographs to support the copy on this topic. I am just as grateful to Avon Tyres Limited, who supplied the photographs relating to motorcycle tyre removal and refitting, and also those that show various forms of tyre damage. Lucas Industries Plc kindly allowed me to reproduce some of their copyright illustrations; I am also much indebted to Castrol (U.K.) Limited who gave advice about their range of lubricants for motorcycles.

The photography accompanying the text is my own and that of Lindsay Porter. It could not have been carried out successfully without his help, advice and assistance, given so willingly.

Robin James, one of this country's leading restorers of classic motorcycles undertook the arduous task of reading and checking my text. His helpful suggestions helped improve its quality. He also provided the front cover illustration and made available some of the machines featured in the photographs. Ken Middleditch and Ken Woodward also kindly made their machines available to photograph. Thanks also to Dave Rosser without whose last minute assistance enabled us to complete our photo sequences.

If I have inadvertently missed anyone else who helped me with this project, my sincere apologies for this unwarranted oversight.

Jeff Clew
Sparkford

Using This Book

Everything about this book is designed to help you make your classic bike more reliable and long-lasting through regular servicing. But one requirement that you will see emphasised again and again is the need for safe working. There is a lot of safety information within the practical instructions but you are strongly urged to read and take note of **Chapter 1, Safety First!**. To get the most from this book, you will rapidly realise that it revolves around two main chapters. **Chapter 3, Service Intervals, Step-by Step,** shows you how to carry out every service task that your motorcycle is likely to need throughout its life. Then, in the final Section, **Service History**, in the back of this book lists all of the tasks described in **Chapter 3** and arranges them together in tick-lists, a separate list for each Service interval, so that you can create your own Service History as you go along.

Keeping your motorcycle in peak condition is one thing; getting it there in the first place may be quite another. At the start of **Chapter 3,** we advise on a 'catch up' service for motorcycles that may not have received the de-luxe treatment suggested here.

Then there are four other chapters to help you acquire a classic motorcycle if you do not already own one, or to help you sell it and replace it with another if that is your wish. **Chapter 4, Buying a Classic Bike** and **Chapter 5, Selling a Classic Bike** show what to look out for when seeking a genuine machine and how to dispose of it satisfactorily when you have decided on a change. These are topics not usually found amongst servicing information but which can help you save money if you buy and sell wisely. **Chapter 6** shows you how to Fault Find when your motorcycle will not start or run correctly and **Chapter 7**, describes getting through the MOT Test successfully, an annual worry - unless you follow the approach suggested here. With **Chapter 2, Buying Spares**, which outlines how you can find those difficult to obtain parts, we hope this book will become the first tool you'll pick up when you want to service your classic bike!

This book is produced in association with Castrol (U.K.) Ltd.

"Motorcycles have become more and more sophisticated. But changing the oil and brake fluid, and similar jobs, are just as simple as ever they were. Castrol are pleased to be associated with this book because it gives us the opportunity to make life simpler for those who wish to service their own motorcycles.
Castrol have succeeded in making oil friendlier and kinder to the environment by removing harmful chlorine from our range of engine lubricants, while noticeably maintaining the engine at its peak efficiency.
In return, we ask you to be kinder to the environment too, by taking your used oil to your Local Authority Amenity Oil Bank. It can then be used as a heating fuel. Please do not poison it with thinners, paint, creosote or brake fluid because these render it useless and costly to dispose of."

Castrol (U.K.) Ltd.

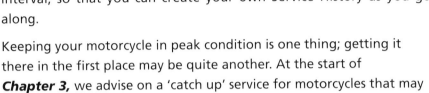

CHAPTER 1 - SAFETY FIRST!

It is vitally important that you always take time to ensure safety is the first consideration in any job you do. A slight lack of concentration, or a rush to finish the job quickly, can often result in an accident, as can failure to take a few simple precautions. Whereas skilled mechanics are trained in safe working practices you, the home mechanic, must find them out for yourself and act upon them.

Remember, accidents don't just happen, they are caused, and some of those causes are outlined in the following list. Above all else, ensure that whenever you work on your motorcycle you adopt a safety-minded approach at all times, and remain aware of the dangers that might be encountered.

Be sure to consult the suppliers of any materials and equipment you may use, and to obtain and read carefully any operating and health and safety instructions that may be available on packaging or from manufacturers and suppliers.

Important Points

ALWAYS ensure that the motorcycle is firmly supported when raised off the ground. Never work on it while it is supported only by its prop stand and even when it is on its centre or rear stand it should have extra support to prevent it from toppling over sideways. Working on it is made easier if it is raised on a workbench, but only if its is firmly anchored to the bed of the workbench by tie downs or some similar supportive means.

NEVER start the engine before checking the gearbox is in neutral. Place a block of some kind in front of, and behind, the front wheel to prevent the machine from moving forward.

NEVER drain off the engine oil when the engine is really hot. Allow sufficient time for it to cool off to avoid being scalded, even though draining is best accomplished while the oil is still warm.

NEVER attempt to loosen or tighten nuts that require a great deal of force to turn them (e.g. a tight engine or gearbox drain plug) while the machine is raised other than on a workbench. Wherever possible, slacken any tight fastenings before raising the machine off the ground.

TAKE CARE to avoid touching any engine or exhaust system component until it is cool enough not to burn you.

ALWAYS keep antifreeze and brake fluid away from any paint-work, instrument or light lenses. Wash off any spills immediately.

NEVER siphon fuel, antifreeze, brake fluid or other similar toxic fluids by mouth, or allow them to have prolonged contact with your skin. There is an increasing awareness that they can damage your health. Best of all, use a suitable hand pump and wear gloves.

1. ALWAYS have a workshop-type of fire extinguisher to hand when working on your machine.

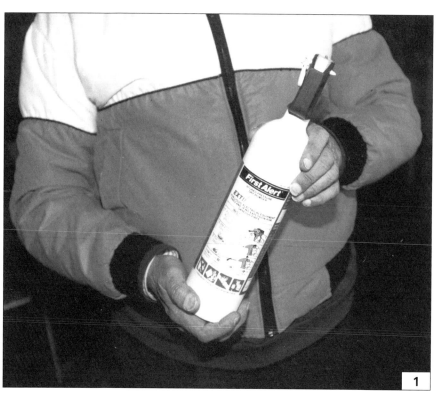

ALWAYS work in a well ventilated area and don't inhale dust - it may contain asbestos or other poisonous substances.

WIPE UP any spilt oil, grease or water off the floor immediately, before there is an accident.

MAKE SURE that spanners and other tools are the right size for the job and are not likely to slip as the result of jaws that have spread. Never try to 'double up' spanners to get better leverage or use tools of doubtful quality.

SEEK HELP if you need to lift something heavy which may be beyond your capability.

ALWAYS ensure that the safe load rating of any workbench you intend using is sufficient for the job, and that it is used only as recommended by the manufacturer.

NEVER take any short cuts or rush to finish a job. Plan ahead and allow plenty of time.

BE meticulous and keep the floor and work area tidy - you'll avoid frustration, work better, and lose less.

KEEP children and animals right away from the work area and unattended machines.

BEFORE undertaking dirty jobs, use a barrier cream on your hands as a protection against infection. Preferably, wear thin gloves, available from D-I-Y outlets.

DON'T lean over, or work on, a running engine unless absolutely necessary, and keep long hair or loose clothing well out of the way of mechanical parts.

DON'T continue working when you are dog tired and no longer thinking correctly. Many difficult jobs will seem much easier after a rest.

REMOVE your wrist watch, rings and all other jewellery before doing any work on the motorcycle, especially when working on the electrical system.

ALWAYS tell someone what you're doing and have them regularly check that all is well, especially when working alone on the machine.

ALWAYS seek specialist advice if you are in doubt about any job. The safety of your motorcycle affects not only you but also your passenger and other road users.

Fire

Petrol (gasoline) is a dangerous and highly flammable liquid requiring special precautions when handling it. When working on the fuel system first disconnect the battery earth (ground) terminal whenever possible and always work outside, or in a well ventilated area. Any form of spark, such as that caused by an electrical fault, by two metal surfaces striking against each other, by a central heating boiler in the garage 'firing up' or

even by static electricity built up in your clothing can, in a confined space, ignite petrol vapour to cause an explosion. Take great care not to spill petrol on to the engine or the exhaust system, never allow any naked flame anywhere near the work area, and above all else, do not smoke.

Invest in a workshop-size fire extinguisher. Choose the carbon dioxide type, or preferably, dry powder, but never a water type extinguisher for workshop use. Water conducts electricity and can make worse an oil or petrol-based fire, in certain circumstances.

Fumes

In addition to the fire hazards described previously, petrol (gasoline) vapour and vapour from many solvents, thinners and adhesives, is highly toxic and under certain conditions can lead to unconsciousness or even death, if inhaled. The risks are increased if such fluids are used in a confined space so always ensure adequate ventilation, or wear a mask, when handling materials of this nature. Treat all such substances with care, always read the instructions, and follow them implicitly.

Always ensure the motorcycle is outside the work place if the engine is running. Exhaust fumes contain poisonous carbon monoxide which will quickly overwhelm the unwary without warning and can kill. Never run the engine with the motorcycle in the garage or in any confined space.

Mains Electricity

Best of all, use rechargeable tools and a DC inspection lamp, powered from a remote 12 volt battery - both are much safer! However, if you do use a mains-powered inspection lamp or power tool etc, ensure that the appliance is wired correctly to its plug, that where necessary it is properly earthed (grounded) and that the fuse is of the correct rating for the appliance concerned. Do not use any mains powered equipment in damp conditions, or in the vicinity of fuel, fuel vapour or the machine's battery.

Also, before using any mains powered equipment, take one more simple precaution - use an RCD (Residual Current Device) circuit breaker. Then, if there is a short circuit, the RCD circuit breaker minimises the risk of electrocution by instantly cutting off the power supply. Buy one from any electrical store or D-I-Y centre. RCDs fit into the electrical socket before you plug in your electrical equipment.

The Ignition System

Extreme care must be taken when working on the ignition system with the engine running or in the case of a coil ignition system, with the ignition switched on.

Touching certain parts of the ignition system, such as the HT leads, distributor cap, ignition coil etc, can result in a severe electric shock. This is especially likely where the insulation on any of these components is poor, or if the components are dirty or damp. Note that the voltages produced by electronic ignition systems are much higher than those of conventional

SAFETY FIRST!

systems and could prove fatal, particularly to persons with cardiac pacemaker implants. Consult the owners handbook or a specialist in your machine's marque if in any doubt; or if the original ignition system has been modified, its supplier. An additional risk of injury can arise while working on a running engine if the operator touches a high voltage lead and pulls a hand away on to a conductive or revolving part.

The Battery

Don't smoke, allow a naked light, or cause a spark near the motorcycle's battery, even in a well ventilated area. A certain amount of explosive hydrogen gas will be given off as part of the normal charging process. Care should be taken to avoid sparking by switching off the power supply before the charger leads are connected or disconnected. Battery terminals should be shielded, since a battery contains stored energy and a spark can be caused by any conductor which touches its terminals or exposed connecting straps.

Before working on the fuel or the electrical system, always disconnect the battery earth (ground) terminal first.

When charging the battery from an external source, disconnect the battery leads before connecting the charger. If the battery is not of the 'sealed for life' type, loosen the filler plugs or remove the cover before charging. For the best results, the battery should be given a low rate 'trickle' charge overnight. Do not charge at an excessive rate or the battery may burst.

Always wear goggles and gloves when carrying or topping up a battery. Even in the diluted form in which it is found in the battery, acid electrolyte is extremely corrosive and must not be allowed to contact the eyes, skin or clothes.

Brakes and Asbestos

2. Whenever you work on the mechanical components of the braking system, or remove the brake shoes or pads:

i) wear an efficient particle mask.

ii) wipe off all brake dust from the work area (never blow it off with compressed air).

iii) dispose of brake dust and discarded linings, shoes or pads in a sealed plastic bag.

iv) wash your hands thoroughly after you have finished working on the brakes, and certainly before you eat or smoke.

v) replace linings, shoes or pads only with today's asbestos-free counterparts. Note that asbestos brake dust can cause cancer, if inhaled.

Obviously a motorcycle's brakes are among its most important safety related items. Do not dismantle your motorcycle's brakes unless you are fully competent to do so. If you have not been trained in this work, but wish to carry out the tasks described

in this book, it is strongly recommended that you have a dealer or a qualified mechanic check your work before you use your motorcycle on the road.

Clutch Linings and Asbestos

Similar advice applies to the linings in a clutch chainwheel or in the individual inserted clutch plates, especially on older machines.

Brake Fluid

While this will be of concern only to those who own a machine fitted with a disc brake or brakes, brake fluid is hygroscopic, which means it absorbs moisture rapidly from the air and can become dangerous, resulting in brake failure. Castrol (U.K.) Ltd. recommend that you should have your brake fluid tested at least once a year by a garage properly equipped with test equipment. You should change the fluid in accordance with your motorcycle manufacturer's recommendations, or as advised in this book if we recommend a shorter interval. Buy no more brake fluid than you will need as it will deteriorate during storage. Never store a pack that has been opened. Dispose of what remains at your Local Authority Waste Disposal Site, in the designated disposal unit, not with the general waste.

Engine Oils

Take care and observe the following precautions when working with used engine oil. Apart from the obvious risk of scalding when draining the oil from a hot engine, there is also danger from contaminates contained in all used oil. Always wear disposable plastic or rubber gloves when draining the oil from your engine.

2

i) Note that the drain plug and the oil are often hotter than you would expect! Wear gloves if the plug is too hot to touch and keep your hand to one side so that you are not scalded by the spurt of oil as the plug comes away.

ii) There are very real health hazards associated with used oil through prolonged and repeated contact, which may cause serious skin disorders, including dermatitis and cancer. Use a barrier cream on your hands and try not to get oil on them. Wear gloves and wash your hands with hand cleaner soon after completing the work. Keep oil out of the reach of children.

iii) NEVER, EVER dispose of old engine oil into the ground or down a drain. In the UK and most EC countries, every local authority must provide a safe means of oil disposal. In the UK, try your local Environmental Health Department for advice about waste disposal facilities.

Plastic Materials

Although only the more modern machines are likely to use plastic materials in their construction, or as fibreglass fairings or enclosures, working with these materials can create additional hazards in the workshop. Many of the materials used (polymers, resins, adhesives and agents such as catalysts and accelerators) readily produce very dangerous situations in the form of poisonous fumes, skin irritants, the risk of fire, and explosions. Do not allow resin or two-pack adhesive hardener, or that supplied with filler or two-pack stopper to come into contact with the skin or eyes. Read carefully the safety notes provided on the can, tube or packaging.

FLUOROELASTOMERS

MOST IMPORTANT! PLEASE READ THIS SECTION!

If you service your motorcycle in the usual way, it is unlikely that any of the following will be relevant to you. Exceptions are likely to occur, however, if your motorcycle has been on fire (even in a localised area), subjected to heat in, say a vehicle breaker's yard, or if any parts have been subjected to repair by heating, such as by brazing or the use of an oxy-acetylene torch.

Many synthetic rubber-like materials used in motorcycles contain a substance called fluorine. These materials are known as fluoroelastomers and are commonly used for oil seals, wiring and cabling, bearing surfaces, gaskets, diaphragms, hoses, 'O' rings and grommets. If they are subjected to temperatures greater than 315 degrees C, they will decompose and can be potentially hazardous. Fluoroelastomer materials will show physical signs of decomposition under such conditions in the form of charred sticky black masses. Some decomposition may occur at lower temperatures, above 200 degrees C, and it is obvious that when a motorcycle has been fire damaged, the fluoroelastomers will decompose in the manner indicated.

In the presence of any water or humidity, including atmospheric moisture, the by-products caused by the fluoroelastomers being heated can be extremely dangerous. According to the Health and Safety Executive "Skin contact with this liquid or decomposition residues can cause painful and penetrating burns. Permanent irreversible skin and tissue damage can occur". Damage can also be caused to eyes or by the inhalation of fumes created as the fluoroelastomers are burned or heated.

After fires or exposure to high temperatures observe the following precautions:

1. Do not touch blackened or charred seals or equipment.

2. Allow all burnt or decomposed fluoroelastomer materials to cool down before inspection, investigations, strip down or removal.

3. Preferably, don't handle parts containing decomposed fluoroelastomers, but if you must, wear goggles and PVC or neoprene protective gloves while doing so. Never handle such parts until they are completely cool.

4. Contaminated parts, residues, materials and clothing, including protective clothing and gloves, should be disposed of by an approved contractor to landfill or incineration according to national or local regulations. Oil seals, gaskets, 'O' rings and grommets, along with contaminated material, must not be burned locally.

Workshop Safety - General

1. Always have a fire extinguisher of the correct type at arm's length when working on the fuel system. If you do have a fire, DON'T PANIC! Use the extinguisher effectively by directing it at the base of the fire. Check frequently whether your fire extinguisher is still in an operable condition. Most have a simple visual means of doing this. Have it checked by a fire extinguisher specialist every year.

2. NEVER use a naked flame near petrol or anywhere in the workplace.

3. KEEP your inspection lamp well away from any source of petrol (gasoline) such as when disconnecting a carburettor float chamber or bowl, fuel lines or a tap.

4. NEVER use petrol (gasoline) to clean parts. Use instead paraffin (kerosene) or white spirits.

5. NO SMOKING! There is always a risk of fire or transmitting dangerous substances to your mouth and, in any case, ash falling into mechanical components is to be avoided.

6. BE METHODICAL in everything you do, use common sense, and think safety at all times. If at all possible, do not break off in the middle of a reassembly sequence, otherwise there is risk of missing out an important stage.

CHAPTER 2 - BUYING SPARES

Although this book will go a long way in ensuring your classic motorcycle has a high standard of reliability there will, of course, be occasions when you will need to buy spare parts to either service it or keep it running. There are still a number of sources of supply of the components necessary when carrying out a service task, their quality and price varying according to the supplier. As with most things in life, cheapest is not necessarily the best, and as a general rule our advice is to put quality before price. It is a policy that usually works out less expensive in the long run! But how can you identify quality? It's sometimes difficult, especially when there are few alternatives available. It is here that reputation needs to be taken into account so stick with parts that have given you dependable service in the past, have been recommended by others, and have well-established brand names. Don't pay over the odds, though! The same parts are often available at widely varying prices from different sources, so if you want to save money, buy wisely by shopping around.

When buying spares, take with you the date of your motorcycle's manufacture and also its engine and frame numbers. These can be helpful when the specification of parts has been changed during production and can be a key to a more helpful approach by some parts salespeople! You may, by now, have entered this key information in the *'Bike Biography* pages at the front of this book, for ease of reference.

Specialist Dealers

Although virtually nothing remains of the old British motorcycle industry, and few of the original concessionaires for machines of foreign manufacture, many of their original dealers and agents still exist. Although some of them may now stock and sell modern motorcycles, and their associated spares, it is possible that they may still hold what remains of the original stock of spare parts for the machines they once represented. Looking through old motorcycling magazines is one way of identifying their link with the past.

Try to avoid giving them a 'shopping list' of parts you need over the telephone, even if you have the original part numbers. It will prove much more successful to visit in one of their quieter periods, and certainly not on a Saturday morning. Remember they now make their money from a new generation of machines and have probably written off their stock of old parts. Be prepared to leave your list with them so that they can look the parts out at their leisure, and don't expect to purchase them at their price in 1954!

The more obscure the make or model, the more difficult it will be to find the

parts you need, other than the more expendable items. There are, however, alternative ways of going about as discussed later in this text.

Parts Factors and Accessory Shops

Generally speaking, this type of shop is geared mainly in favour of the motorist. They are still worth investigating, however, as many items common to both cars and motorcycles can often be obtained at advantageous prices. They are likely to be open for longer hours too, especially at weekends.

Oil, grease, sparking plugs, bulbs and similar items are invariably available at these shops, along with workshop tools and similar garage equipment.

One-Make Specialists

The owner of a classic motorcycle is almost certain to know the name, address and telephone number of dealers who specialise only in the make of machine they own. If in any doubt, details will be found without difficulty in any of the classic motorcycling magazines or tabloids. This category of dealer will have a tremendous amount of expertise at their disposal and even if their stock of parts has diminished dramatically over the years, they will know where parts are likely to be found or may even have had some made to the maker's original specification. All are fiercely loyal to the make of machine for which they once held the agency, so this is not the place to make disparaging remarks (or mention Japanese motorcycles!).

Repair work beyond the capability of the average D-I-Y mechanic can safely be entrusted to these specialists, in the knowledge that they will take pride in their high standard of workmanship. Furthermore, they are likely to have a full set of

the original factory service tools. Bear in mind that craftsmanship does not come cheap, so be prepared to pay the going rate in the knowledge you are getting the best possible attention. If in doubt, you can always ask for an estimate first. Some will offer parts or service at a discounted rate if you are a member of the club that caters for the marque in which they specialise.

Similar advice applies to that given under the Specialist Dealer heading when you have a 'shopping list' of the spare parts you need. It helps considerably if you can quote the original parts numbers as this category of dealer is likely to have an unfailing memory and an almost total recall of part numbers. If you have made a mistake in either your description of a part or its number, they are likely to spot it and raise a query!

Clubs

Any classic motorcycle owner will find it pays dividends to become a member of the one-make club that specialises in the make of machine they own. Many have their own spares organisation, with the ability to have replica parts specially made to the maker's original specification assuming there is sufficient demand. Inevitably these will prove costly because it is much more expensive to make replica parts in small batches rather than in large numbers.

Each one-make club will also have its own magazine, which will contain features of interest to owners and allow an inter-

change of ideas through its correspondence pages. A fortunate few now hold the manufacturer's original service records, so that the year of manufacture of any machine can be firmly established. This is of particular importance where a machine is not recorded on the Swansea computer and no longer has any officially recognised registration numbers. The DVLC now recognises many of the one-make clubs as an authoritative source for dating a machine and verifying its authenticity so that an age-related registration number can be allocated where none exists.

1. Also worthy of consideration is becoming a member of the Vintage Motor Cycle Club Ltd, a club with a world-wide membership of around 12,000. It caters for any machine, British or foreign, that is more than 25 years old and runs a wide variety of events of both the on- and off-road type. Local Sections look after the needs of members in virtually every part of the country, each with its own officials who are responsible to the main committee of the club.

Advantages of membership are many. The club has its own headquarters in the Midlands, with an extensive library that now contains the service records of many of the old manufacturers. A panel of Marque Specialists is also available to give free of charge advice to bona fide members about any problem they may encounter with a particular make of machine. Other services include a machine dating service, and assistance to help retain original registration numbers not on the Swansea computer, both services being recognised by the DVLC. The club also has an excellent monthly magazine The Vintage Motor Cycle and a Machine Register which serves as an excellent guide to the dating of a machine by reference to its frame and engine numbers.

Pattern Parts Manufacturers and Stockists

The quite remarkable and ever-growing amount of interest shown in classic motorcycles during the last couple of decades has resulted in the manufacture of spare parts that are replicas of the originals. With virtually none of the old motorcycle manufacturers still in business, parts they once bought-in are now becoming available through their original sub-contractors. Mostly for sale indirectly through a number of different outlets, they are of dependable and sometimes of improved quality as the result of advances in manufacturing techniques or the use of better quality materials. Most important of all they will fit exactly, without need for any modification. Prices under these circumstances may seem high, but one has to remember that they are now made in much smaller quantity. Quality never comes cheaply.

Inevitably there is someone who will cut corners to achieve a greater profit margin. However, these 'rogue' parts may appear indistinguishable from the genuine replacement part, and they are sometimes difficult to detect. It is only through personal recommendations (and dire warnings!) that you can be sure of buying wisely. Crankpins that break within a few hundred miles because they have been incorrectly machined or hardened are by no means uncommon. Nor are exhaust systems where nothing lines up and any attempt at further bending will destroy the already thin layer of flashed-on plating.

Buying Secondhand

Autojumbles (rather a misnomer when they relate to motorcycle parts!) are now the main source of supply for the more obscure makes and models of classic motorcycle. Special care needs to be exercised here, not only in being able to identify the part that is exactly correct but also in making sure it is not badly worn or damaged in any way.

We strongly advise against buying secondhand frames, forks, suspension and brake components unless the source of the parts is known and it is evident they are in first class condition. Parts from a crash damaged or burnt out motorcycle should be viewed with grave suspicion - it is your life that will be at risk.

It is particularly difficult to find carburettors that are anything but badly worn, even if you are fortunate enough to find one of exactly the correct type specified for your model. There is an infinite variety of different types, with varying choke sizes, differing downdraught angles and jet blocks specified for a particular make and model of machine. It does not follow that one which looks right is necessarily a suitable replacement. If you find the carburettor you desperately need to get your machine running, check the fit of the slide in the mixing chamber body and in relation to the jet block. Check also for stripped threads, distortion by over-tightening and cracks. Air leaks create erratic running and take the edge off performance, as well as play havoc with fuel consumption.

In the case of distributors it is easy to check whether the main spindle can be waggled about, a sure sign of badly worn bearings. This will affect the correct setting of the contact breaker points and make it impossible to set the ignition timing correctly. Wear is often the main problem with most secondhand parts, and is not easy to detect without accurate measuring equipment.

Whenever possible, to take with you the part or parts that need replacing. It is surprising how many buy parts which they are sure are identical to the part left at home, only to find subsequently that it differs in various respects and is quite unsuitable.

Checks on Running Gear Components

Although many outlets sell 'reconditioned' components on an 'exchange' basis, the quality of workmanship and the extent to which the component has been reconditioned can vary greatly. A fresh coat of paint means little, so always check carefully before buying. It follows that reconditioned components are best obtained from main agents or from reputable specialist suppliers. This is another area where personal recommendations count for much, especially as this area applies largely to electrical components.

Brakes (NEW parts ONLY!)

Look for boxes bearing genuine manufacturer's labels, such as Ferodo, Fibrax and similar with respect to brake linings. Make sure you obtain the type of lining that is best suited to your machine and the way it is used. Racing linings are of little use on a machine to be ridden on the road, especially a lightweight two-stroke. Conversely, if a 'soft' lining is used on a machine with sporting pretensions, continuous hard application of the brakes will result in brake fade.

More modern linings are bonded directly to the brake shoe, as distinct from being riveted on. The strength of the bond is all important so check carefully for any signs of lifting. *Buy asbestos-free whenever available*

Brake pads need to be selected with similar care. Whenever possible, use what the manufacturer recommended or a later type of known quality.

Suspension

Telescopic front forks must be straight, have both legs exactly in line with one another and move freely. They are the first parts to suffer damage in any head-on accident. Check also the effectiveness of the damping, assuming they still contain oil. Note, however, that most lightweight-model forks have no provision for damping.

Dowty 'Oleomatic' front forks are sometimes seen. They have no internal springs and rely solely on their air content as the suspension medium. Buy with caution, even if they were originally specified for the machine you own. Their seals are almost impossible to obtain and if the sliders happen to be scratched, the slow leakage of air will be inevitable. A spring conversion is the only really suitable option.

Don't forget to check the condition of the steering head races. If they are rusty or the bearing track is pitted, they will need to be renewed along with the cups in the steering head of the machine's frame. Check also for worn bushes in the slider assemblies. Although the bushes can be renewed, excessive play here is one of the main causes of a machine failing the MoT test.

Rear suspension units lead a hard life and the later types cannot be taken apart to be reconditioned. Check whether they still have any damping action and look for fluid leakages. Whenever possible, buy new rather than secondhand replacements. This advice applies equally well to the suspension units of Earles-type front forks.

Tyres

Tyres may create the biggest problem of all, as many of the old sizes are no longer available. Often, the easiest way around this problem is to have the wheels built on rims of a different size for which modern tyres are readily available - with the proviso that the wheel size differs only to a very minor extent. Modern tyres are much safer due to advances in rubber technology. They will hold the road better and prove far safer in the wet.

In some instances, cheaper tyres are available from the Far East, but beware if the supplier asks you whether the machine is for display only. Some will give a distinctly odd handling effect and prove absolutely lethal in the wet. Buy wisely and fit a well-known brand.

Secondhand tyres often offer an attractive alternative, and may be the only option if that size and/or type of tread is no longer available. Unfortunately such tyres may have hidden faults, even if they are still in their original wrappers and appear to have stored well.

The way in which a tyre ages depends very much on how it has been stored, so if you are willing to accept the risk do make sure you examine the tyre carefully before you buy.

2. Look for cracks in the sidewalls and tread blocks or pattern, however small, and make sure the tyre itself is still pliable.

Reject it if any of these faults are evident or if there are any other blemishes, especially uneven wear. Remoulds in motorcycle sizes are rarely seen, but if they are, reject them too. To use them is false economy as you have too much to lose should they fail while in use. An RQ stamped on the sidewall of a tyre denotes 'remould quality'.

Our advice, very strongly given, is to stick to top quality, unused tyres from a reputable manufacturer, even if you have to change a rim size to suit. New tyres may cost a little more, but at least you will have peace of mind and will be able to ride in all road and weather conditions with confidence. Your own life and that of other road users may well depend on it.

Saving Money

Finally, if you want to buy quality and save money you must be prepared to shop around. Ring each of your suppliers with a list of your requirements and your motorcycle's personal data from the Bike Biography at the front of this book in front of you. Keep a written note of prices, whether the parts have well-recognised brand-names or not. Most importantly of all, check whether or not the parts you need are in stock. Parts on back order or 'expected soon' have been known never to materialise!

Locating Frame and Engine Numbers

Motorcycle manufacturers have not until recent years standardised a common location for their frame and engine numbers, modern machines having a readily evident VIN (Vehicle Identification Number) plate on which both are stamped. On older motorcycles, especially with regard to the frame number, they can be found almost anywhere!

3. The most common frame number location is on or close to the steering head lug, either across it or at the joint with the front down tube(s) of the frame.

BUYING SPARES

4. Alternative locations are on the lug under the saddle...

...on one of the horizontal engine plate mounting lugs, or above the gearbox.

Do not confuse the frame number with a manufacturer's part number. A frame number is invariably stamped on, whereas a part number is usually cast-in and raised as though it had been embossed. A number may be particularly hard to find on a frame that has been completely re-enamelled and has filled in.

5. The engine number is usually more easily found, as it is common practice to stamp it on the nearside mouth of the crankcase, immediately below the cylinder barrel. It can, however, sometimes be found in a similar location on the offside, or on the top of the crankcase, behind the cylinder barrel. Villiers engines have their engine number stamped on a plate attached to the primary chaincase - not a good idea as chaincases sometimes have to be changed.

Some manufacturers, such as Triumph, always used identical frame and engine numbers, while others matched them at random. Engine numbers often include the model identification number in their code, while AJS and Matchless also incorporate the year of manufacture. The numbers or letters before or after an engine number are just as important as the engine number itself for correct identification purposes, so make sure you always give the complete number.

4

Gearbox numbers are usually stamped on either the gearbox shell or the end cover. If the engine is built on unit-construction lines, a number is unlikely to be found. Sometimes an additional code number is evident, such as RRT2 on a BSA 'Gold Star' gearbox. In this case it denotes a close ratio gearbox, suitable for racing purposes. It is, of course, possible to change the gearbox internals without altering the code.

5

CHAPTER 3
SERVICE INTERVALS, STEP BY STEP

Everyone would like to own a motorcycle that starts first kick, runs reliably and lasts longer than average. Yet there's no magic about how to put your motorcycle into that category; it's all a question of thorough maintenance! If you follow the Service Jobs listed here - or have a motorcycle dealer or mechanic do it for you, you can almost guarantee that your motorcycle will still be going when others have fallen by the wayside....or stopped on the hard shoulder. Mind you, we would be among the first to acknowledge that this Service Schedule is just about as thorough as you can get. It's an amalgam of all the maker's recommended service items, be it a four-stroke or a two-stroke, plus all the 'inside information from the experts we have consulted. If you want your motorcycle to be as well looked after as possible, you'll follow the jobs shown here, but if you don't want to go the whole way, you can pick and choose from the most essential items on the list. Do bear in mind, however, that the jobs we recommend are listed for some very good reasons:

◆ *preventative maintenance* figures very high on our list of priorities. That's why so many of our service jobs have the word "Check..." near the start.

◆ *older motorcycles* need more attention than their modern counterparts; it's as simple as that - so we have listed the jobs you will need to carry out in order to keep any motorcycle within the coverage of this book in fine fettle.

◆ *remember* that if you use your motorcycle infrequently or only for a series of short journeys, it is advisable to service it more frequently. This also applies if it is ridden at high speeds or in particularly dry and dusty conditions.

USING THE SERVICE SCHEDULES

At the start of each Service Job you'll see a heading in bold type, looking a bit like this:

☐ **Job 13. Change engine oil**

Following the heading will be all the information you will need to enable you to carry out that particular job. Please note that different makes and models of motorcycle may have different requirements regarding quantities. Please check with the manufacturer's recommendations. Exactly the same Job number will be found in *Appendix 4, Service History*, found at the back of this book. Here you will want to keep a complete record of all the work you have carried out. After you have finished servicing your motorcycle, you will be able to tick off all the jobs you have completed and

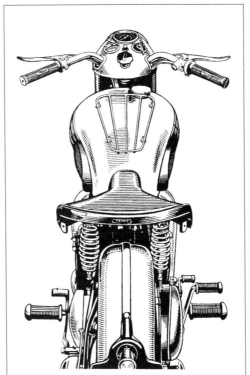

The controls: a typical layout.

so, service by service, build up a complete Service History of work completed on your motorcycle during your period of ownership.

You will also find key information immediately above each Job title and in most cases there will be reference to an illustration - a photograph or a line drawing, whichever is the easier for you to follow - usually on the same page.

If the Job applies only to a certain type of motorcycle, the Job title will be followed by a description of the motorcycle to which the Job title applies. For instance, Job 13 applies to a four-stroke and the information that follows tells you so.

Two other special headings are also used. One reads **OPTIONAL**, which means you can use your own discretion whether to carry out this particular Job or whether to leave it until it occurs again in a later service. The other is INSIDE INFORMA-TION. This tells you that there is a Job or a special tip that you wouldn't normally get to hear about, other than through experience and the 'inside' knowledge of the experts who have helped with the compilation of this Service Guide. On rare occasions, we recommend you have work carried out by a specialist: where we believe you may be better off having the work done for you, we say so, using the term, SPECIALIST SERVICE.

SAFETY FIRST!
The other special heading is the one that could be the most important of all - SAFETY FIRST! In addition, please read Chapter 1 Safety First! at the beginning of this book before carrying out any work on your motorcycle.

Throughout the Service Schedule, each 'shorter' Service interval becomes an important part of each of the next 'longer' Service Intervals too. For instance, under the 1,500 mile Service you are instructed to check the tyres for wear or damage. This Job also has to be carried out at 3,000 miles, 6,000 miles, 9,000 miles and so on. It is therefore shown in the list as extra Jobs to be carried out for each of these 'longer' Service Intervals, but only as a Job number. The detailed instructions given the first time around are not repeated.

The 'Catch-up' Service

When you first buy a used motorcycle you never know for sure how well it has been looked after. Even with a full service history (rarely available) it is unlikely to have been serviced as thoroughly as one with a Porter Publishing Service Guide History! So, if you want to catch up on all the servicing that may have been neglected on the motorcycle you now own, just work methodically through the entire list of Service Jobs listed for the *18,000 miles - or Every Thirty Six Months* Service. add on the *Longer Term Servicing* Jobs, and your motorcycle will be brought right up to date and serviced as well as you could hope for. Allow several days for all of this work, not the least because it will almost certainly throw up a number of extra jobs - potential faults that may have been lurking beneath the surface - all of which will need putting right before you can 'sign off' your motorcycle, in the knowledge that it is now in tip-top condition.

Steadying a Motorcycle Safely

I. Unlike a car, you will not need to raise a motorcycle off the ground, unless you use a hydraulic or a winched-up workbench to make working on it much easier. If you do, make sure the safe working load of the workbench is more than sufficient to accommodate the overall weight of the bike and that once the bike is raised, the workbench cannot be lowered accidentally.

Also ensure the motorcycle is anchored securely to the bed of the workbench so that it cannot move forwards or backwards, or tilt sideways. Never use the prop stand to support it in any way. If you intend to rest it on its centre or rear stand, place a piece of carpet under the stand first. This will ensure the

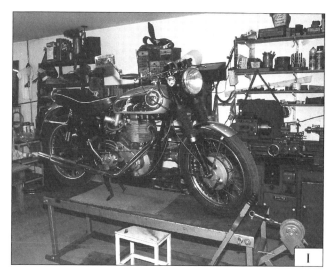

stand does not skid about when the motorcycle is either raised or lowered on to its own stand while on the workbench bed. If the motorcycle is raised off the ground, make sure the surface on which it is to stand is both level and firm. Block the front wheel so that it cannot roll forward, off the stand, and place some strong boxes or similar supports under the footrests (provided they are not of the folding type!) or beneath the crankcase. The end result can be just as dangerous if the machine topples sideways.

When the work is finished, lower the workbench slowly before you remove the tie downs used to anchor the motorcycle. If it has been raised on the ground, remove the supporting boxes and the blocks at the front wheel. Check the gearbox is in neutral before lowering it off its stand in either case.

Daily (before use) Check

A motorcycle, especially a classic motorcycle, deserves to be given a quick check to be sure it is safe and legal to use on the road before it is ridden. Each of the following checks is recommended:

Engine oil level

FOUR-STROKE ENGINES ONLY

II. Check the content of the oil tank or oil compartment in the crankcase. If the oil level appears to be a little low, start the engine and run it for a few seconds so that any oil that may have found its way into the crankcase is returned by the oil pump.

III

IV

Some machines 'wet sump' when unused for a while, resulting in a slow build-up of oil in the crankcase due to oil draining through the oil pump. Stop the engine and check again. If the oil level is still low, add sufficient oil of the correct viscosity to bring it to the required level, usually about an inch below the top of the tank or oil compartment. DO NOT OVERFILL, otherwise oil spillage is bound to occur from the filler cap as the oil warms up and expands in volume. Always check that oil returns to the oil tank or oil compartment when the engine is started, or if fitted that the oil tell-tale or pressure gauge registers.

III. Some machines have a car-type dipstick which makes checking the oil level much easier.

IV. Wipe the dipstick first with a clean rag before checking the level.

V. This type is withdrawn after slipping a retaining clip out of the way before withdrawing it.

Whatever method is used, make sure the machine is standing on level ground and always check BEFORE, not AFTER a run.

TWO-STROKES ONLY

Most two-strokes (such as those fitted with a Villiers engine) run on a petroil mix, so you will have to add a pre-determined amount of oil to the petrol. The alternative is to fill up with premix from a special dispenser, set to deliver the correct ready-mixed ratio of petrol and oil. In such cases, no separate oil check can be made.

V

Other two-strokes, such as a Scott, have either a separate oil compartment in the petrol tank or an oil tank. Oil from either is fed by gravity to a mechanical oil pump and the excess burnt, to be expelled with the exhaust gases. It is not returned to the oil compartment or tank as it would be in a four-stroke. Make sure the compartment or tank is kept full, if it runs dry, serious mechanical damage is inevitable.

Petrol (gasoline)

Make sure the petrol (gasoline) tank holds more than enough for your journey. Although most machines have a reserve, it is usually only sufficient for a few miles, to get you to the nearest filling station - there used to be more of them!

Brakes

Check that the front and rear brakes operate correctly and do not lock in the 'on' position. If your machine has a front disc brake, or disc brakes front and rear, check the hydraulic fluid level in each reservoir to ensure it is not near the minimum level mark.

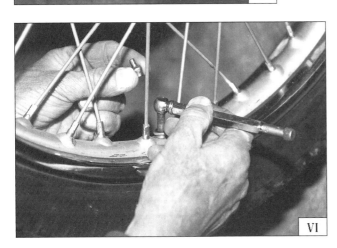

VI

Tyres

VI. Check the tyre pressures while the tyres are still cold, so that you get a correct reading. The pressure gauge used should be one of known accuracy.

VII. While you're in the vicinity, check to ensure that the tyre is not creeping round the rim. The valve should not be at an angle, as it is here. If it is, the tyre will have to be relocated otherwise the tyre valve will be torn out of the inner tube - see later in this chapter.

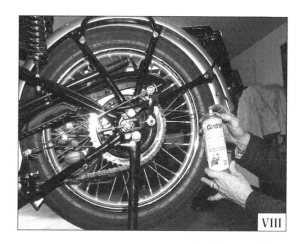

The Final Drive Chain

VIII. Check that the final drive chain is correctly tensioned - there should be three quarters of an inch free up and down movement. Check also that it is well lubricated and that the connecting spring link has not become displaced. In bad weather, the chain is likely to require more frequent attention to keep it from running dry.

IX. Machines fitted with shaft final drive are unlikely to require a daily check unless there are visible signs of oil leakage indicating urgent attention is necessary.

Controls, Cables, and Steering

X. All of the handlebar controls should operate smoothly within their full range and should be fastened securely. This also applies to the kickstarter and gearchange pedals. If the bolt securing the latter unscrews, it can fall off its splines when the machine is in motion and render the machine unrideable.

The brake cable(s) should already have been checked. Check also all of the other control cables for similar faults.

The handlebars should turn smoothly from lock to lock. If the steering head adjustment is too tight, the machine will be inclined to roll, whereas if it is too loose, the forks will judder when the front wheel hits a bump or when the front brake is applied hard. Make sure movement is not restricted by badly routed control cables.

Lights, Horn, and Speedometer

Make sure all of the lights function correctly, including the stop light and the light that illuminates the speedometer. Check the operation of the dip switch. A correctly operating speedometer and horn are both legal requirements.

XI. If the machine is a competition model with no lights, it must be fitted with a bulb horn in working order as an alternative.

500 Miles, Monthly, or Before Long Journeys, Whichever Comes First

These are regular checks you need to carry out, in addition to the daily (before use) check, to ensure your classic motorcycle is safe and reliable. They do not include any major Service Jobs, but they need to be carried out as an integral part of every 'proper' service.

☐ **Job 1. Engine oil level.**

1. Check the level of the oil in the oil tank or in the oil compartment within the crankcase as described previously in the Daily (before use) Check. If the machine is a two-stroke with an independent oil supply to the engine, the oil tank or compartment MUST be kept full. It's a good idea to check that the drain plug is tight too!

☐ **Job 2. Clutch adjustment.**

2A. It is important that there is a small amount of free play at the handlebar lever before the clutch begins to disengage. Make sure there is a minimum of 3/16 in. between the butt of the lever and the handlebar-mounted cable clamp (although Triumph recommend 1/16 in., so check your handbook).

2B. Fine adjustment can be made by means of the cable adjuster at the gearbox, as shown on this Triumph (arrowed) or if there is one fitted, at the handlebar lever itself.

2C. With the inspection cap removed, you can ensure that there is about 1/32 in. of free movement at the clutch rod. Take care not to damage the cast lug! (Illustration, courtesy Triumph)

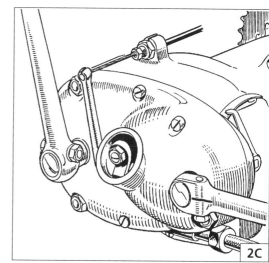

2C

2D. The critical factor is the angle of the arm that presses on the clutch push rod to disengage the clutch. Its own separate means of adjustment may be found externally, or internally via a detachable cover on the gearbox end. Too great an angle will place a sideways stress on the clutch push rod, whereas too small an angle will result in lost leverage and heavier than usual clutch operation. Ideally, the operating lever should be parallel to the face of the gearbox as the clutch commences to disengage. This can be regarded as a coarse adjustment, the cable adjuster subsequently being used to get the clearance adjustment correct.

INSIDE INFORMATION: The design of the Velocette clutch on the larger capacity four-strokes and its mode of operation is quite different from that of any other motorcycle. As a result, this clutch cannot be adjusted in the conventional manner. The special routine described in the manufacturers instructions has to be followed EXACTLY, otherwise it is almost certain you will end up with a clutch that drags and slips simultaneously! Consult your Velocette handbook.

2D

☐ **Job 3. Battery electrolyte.**

SAFETY FIRST!
i) The gas (hydrogen) given off by a battery is highly explosive. Never smoke, use a naked flame or allow a spark to occur in the vicinity of the battery. Never disconnect the battery leads (it can cause sparking) when the vent caps or cover have been removed. ii) Batteries contain sulphuric acid. If the acid comes into contact with the skin or eyes, wash immediately with copious amounts of cold water and seek medical advice. iii) Do not check the electrolyte level within half an hour of the battery being charged by a battery charger or the machine being used. Topping up with fresh water could then cause the highly corrosive electrolyte to flood out of the battery.

3A

3A. On many classic motorcycles the battery is exposed, resting on a platform attached to the frame and retained in position by a clamp. Some of the later models will have it enclosed within a compartment below the seat which may also contain the tool kit, or within a compartment beneath the hinged dual seat.

3B. Release the battery from its clamp and if it is within an enclosed compartment, detach both leads. The vent caps or cover can then be removed once the battery has been lifted out of its compartment. If it is exposed and one of the old type, with a hard black rubber case, removing the detachable lid once the securing clamp has been undone will usually suffice to gain access to the vent caps. Make sure the top half of the clamp does not drop across the exposed ties between the individual cells and cause a spark or a short circuit.

3C. A modern battery will have a translucent plastic case, which permits the electrolyte level to be seen from the outside. It may also have an electrolyte level mark. The electrolyte level in an old black battery can be checked only by shining a torch inside the case, through the now open orifices into which the vent caps screw. When the level is correct, it will be just above each set of plates when the battery is level.

3D. If the electrolyte level is low, top up to the correct level to keep the plates covered, using only distilled or demineralised water, NEVER with tap water.

INSIDE INFORMATION: Do not overfill or the highly corrosive acid will begin to flood out during charging. Wipe any surplus water from the top of the battery and if the terminals show signs of corrosion, take remedial action as described in Job 38.

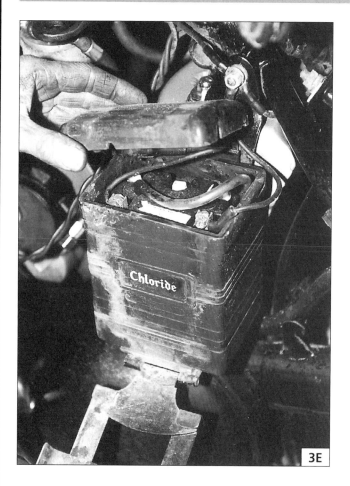

3E

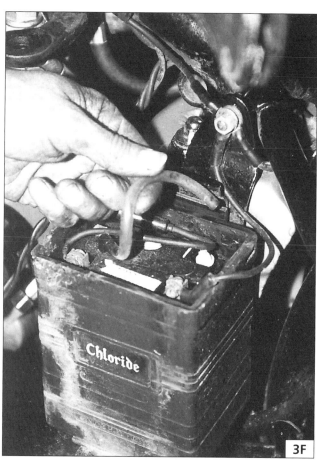

3F

3E. Replace the vent caps or cover, then reconnect the leads, ensuring each is connected to its correct terminal. Not every motorcycle has a negative earth (ground). Place the battery back inside its compartment if of the enclosed type, or refit the lid if it is exposed, and tighten the retaining clamp.

3F. If the battery has a vent pipe, check that the pipe is correctly routed so that no part of it is squeezed or trapped. Make sure it does not discharge on to paintwork or any chromium plating. In either case the acid vapour will quickly strip the protective coating and corrode the bare metal below.

3G. INSIDE INFORMATION: Old 'T' type batteries are no longer available and it is sometimes difficult to find even standard black rubber case batteries to replace them. But a solution is at hand...

3G

3H. If you wish to preserve the original appearance of your machine, find a discarded battery of the correct type, hollow it out after first draining the acid and flush it out with copious amounts of water. When it has dried out, a smaller battery of the type made by most Japanese battery manufacturers can then be slipped inside and connected up, its presence completely concealed. Be sure to only dispose of the old acid at your local authority disposal point - or consult your local garage for their advice.

An alternative is to purchase a replica outer case of the old battery moulded in fibreglass, virtually indistinguishable from the original, and use it in a similar manner.

3H

4A

Job 4. Coolant system

The majority of classic motorcycles have an air-cooled engine, but there are exceptions such as the model LE Velocette and the Scott. These systems work on the thermo-siphon system and do not have either a water pump or a thermostat.

4A. Make a visual check of the system, looking particularly for leaks from any of the hose joints or from the radiator core.

4B

4B. Top up if necessary with a 50% mixture of anti-freeze and water until the coolant level is just below the filler cap. Irrespective of climatic conditions, it is advisable to keep the system filled with an anti-freeze mixture of this strength as the anti-freeze contains an inhibitor that will prevent internal corrosion of the water passages throughout the engine.

INSIDE INFORMATION: Anti-freeze is particularly valuable where an engine has a cast iron cylinder barrel and an aluminium alloy cylinder head. These dis-similar metals will create engine-wrecking corrosion without use of the recommended anti-freeze mixture.

SAFETY FIRST!
i) Always check the coolant level WHEN THE SYSTEM IS COLD. Hot water can scald badly. ii) Take precautions to prevent anti-freeze coming into contact with the skin or eyes. If this should happen, rinse immediately with plenty of water and if necessary, seek immediate medical assistance.

5A

☐ Job 5. Chain adjustment, wheel alignment and lubrication.

ADJUSTING PRIMARY CHAIN TENSION

IMPORTANT NOTE: Also see Job 7H: the brake stop light will also almost certainly need adjustment.

5A. Check the tension of the primary chain by removing the inspection cap or cover in the primary chaincase.

5B

INSIDE INFORMATION: You may need to use a piece of flat steel as a 'screwdriver' because a conventional screwdriver will damage this type of slotted cap.

5B. The primary chain should have no more than half an inch up and down play at its tightest point when measured in the middle of its upper or lower run.

5C. If you're not sure what you're looking for, or if you need to check the condition of the chain, you will need to remove the chain cover after draining off the oil. See *Job 22.*

INSIDE INFORMATION: Turn the engine over several times so that the chain's tension can be checked in a number of different positions.

5C

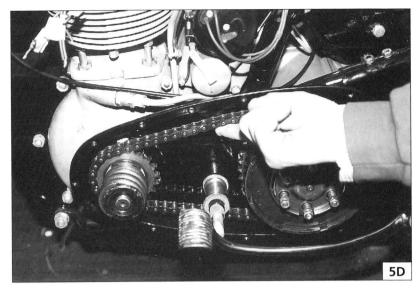

5D

5D. Chains never wear evenly. If the chain is not of the endless type, make sure the spring clip that joins both ends is firmly in position, with its closed end facing the direction in which the chain is travelling.

5E. Because it is not possible to move the gearbox in relation to the engine in a unit-construction design, a Weller tensioner is used to take up primary chain slack. The adjuster is external and below the chaincase, as shown here. Some Villiers engines are of semi-unit construction, having the separate gearbox bolted to the back of the engine. In such cases, primary chain slack is taken up by adding gaskets between the engine and gearbox.

5F. INSIDE INFORMATION: On some models, you may have to remove the footrest and spindle. Always pull the gearbox back after adjusting.

5G. In the accompanying diagram, nuts A will have to be slackened and the drawbolt B used to move the gearbox backwards or forwards. Don't forget to re-tighten the nuts afterwards and re-adjust the final drive chain tension! IMPORTANT NOTE: If you fail to slacken the clamp bolt nut or the gearbox pivot bolt, the gearbox casing may be fractured.

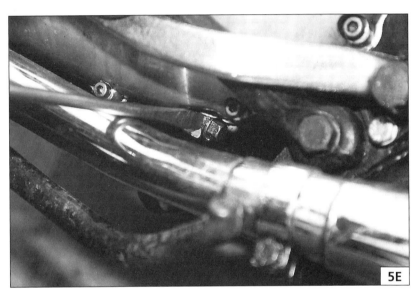

5E

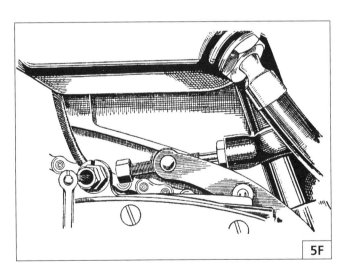

5F

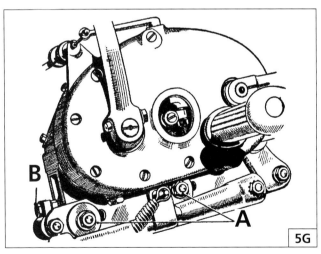

5G

SAFETY FIRST!
DO NOT UNDER ANY CIRCUMSTANCES check the chain tension with the engine running or when someone else is turning it over by the kickstarter. This is a sure way to lose fingers.

5H. Also check the level of the oil in the primary chaincase. Most chaincases leak and it is important that the lower run of the chain remains immersed or rapid wear of the sprockets and chain are bound to follow. Some machines have a level plug to ensure the level is correct. Do not overfill and be sure to use oil of the viscosity recommended by the manufacturer. Triumphs are one of several makes of motorcycle particularly sensitive to chaincase oil viscosity. A grade that is too heavy will cause clutch drag and may even gum up the plates.

ADJUST FINAL DRIVE CHAIN TENSION

5I. Secondary or final drive chains lead a much harder life, most being protected by only a somewhat primitive chainguard. Yours is likely to require more frequent attention. The tension is correct when there is 3/4 in. up and down play in the middle of its top or bottom run when the chain is at its tightest point.

On a machine fitted with either plunger or swinging-arm rear suspension, the chain tension will need to be checked according to the manufacturer's recommendations. This is usually with the rider seated on the machine, or while it is standing with both wheels on the ground. If the machine is on its centre stand, the amount of acceptable play may need to be increased to between 1 1/4 and 1 1/2 ins. Check also that the spring link joining both ends is correctly located and has its closed end facing the direction of the chain's travel.

5J. Adjustment is made by placing the machine on its central or rear stand and slackening the wheel nuts and the nut(s) or bolt securing the rear brake torque arm, if fitted.

5K. Some machines have independent adjusters either side of the wheel...

5L. ...while others have 'snail' cams that ensure the wheel always moves parallel to the frame tubes. Before tightening the wheel nuts, check that the wheel is central in the frame.

ADJUST WHEEL ALIGNMENT

5M. To ensure the wheel alignment is correct after chain adjustment on either a solo or a sidecar outfit, draw two parallel chalked lines either side of the machine to serve as a reliable guide. Alternatively, rest two planks of wood against both side-walls of each tyre, assuming the tyres are of identical size. Adjust the rear wheel by means of the chain adjusters if they are of the separate type. If of the snail cam type, wheel alignment should be correct automatically. Recheck the final drive chain tension if the position of the rear wheel has been changed, before tightening the wheel nuts. Re-adjust the rear brake, if necessary.

ADJUST SIDECAR ALIGNMENT

To check the alignment of a sidecar wheel leave the machine in position against the first board and place another similar board on the floor, touching the outer wall of the sidecar tyre as shown. Measure the distance 'Y' on the sketch, as close to the rear tyres as possible. Measure the distance 'X' in a similar manner, as close to the front tyre as possible. The distance 'X' should be about 3/8 in. less than 'Y' to give suitable "toe-in". If the "toe-in" exceeds 3/8 in. or if there is a "toe-out", rapid tread wear will result.

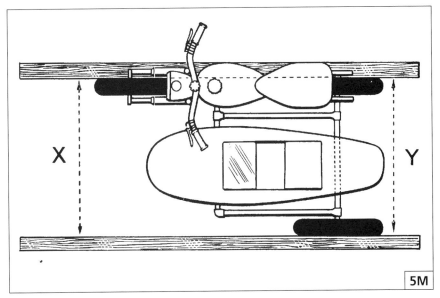

5N. Next check whether the machine is standing upright. This may often be judged by eye but to make certain the following method may be used:

Take a similar board and rest it on a chosen point towards the top of the front fork. Mark the point on the ground where the other end touches. Then do the same with the board moved to the other side of the fork. The distances from each of these marks to the centre line of the tyre should be equal. If they are not the combination is not upright and rapid tread wear will take place.

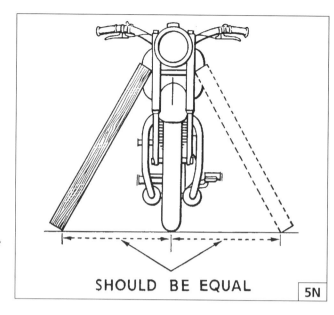

SHOULD BE EQUAL

5N

5O. SAFETY FIRST!
Don't forget to tighten the rear brake torque arm nuts - or bolt as shown here - if a torque arm is fitted. If the torque arm comes adrift, the brake will lock on when it is next applied and the resulting skid can cause a serious accident.

The primary chain is unlikely to require any additional attention as it will have had its lower run immersed in lubricant within the primary chaincase, provided that the correct oil level has been maintained.

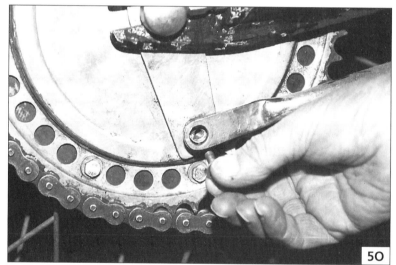

5O

5P. The secondary or final drive chain will require much more frequent attention, especially when the machine is used in wet or very dry and dusty conditions.

To lubricate the chain without having to remove it, first wipe it clean of any water or dust, then apply one of the proprietary aerosol-type chain lubricants. Spray the lubricant on while slowly revolving the wheel, using the small bore plastic tube provided. Apply the lubricant to the inside of the chain so that it can centrifuge outwards. Leave the lubricant to dry for a few minutes before using the machine.

5P

6A

Job 6. Check tyre pressures.

6A. Spin both wheels and check that each tyre is straight on the wheel rim. The circular line moulded in a tyre's sidewall should be equidistant from the wheel rim all the way round.

Check the tyre pressures BEFORE the machine is ridden. Use a tyre pressure gauge that is known to be accurate. If a pillion passenger is to be carried, raise the rear tyre pressure according to the machine's or the tyre manufacturer's recommendations.

Make sure the end cap is replaced on the tyre valve after checking the pressure. The cap (provided it is not of the plastic type) will have a secondary internal rubber seal, useful as a means of slowing deflation. It is rumoured that at very high speeds it has been known for an unprotected tyre valve to leak air and cause the tyre to deflate due to centrifugal force overcoming the strength of its spring-loaded seal. In any case, a seal of some kind is desirable to keep out dirt, which may also hold the valve off its seat.

6B

6B. INSIDE INFORMATION: A rubber sleeve fitted over the exposed valve threads will protect them and make it easier to unscrew the locking ring in the event of a puncture.

Job 7. Adjust/check drum or disc brakes.

SAFETY FIRST! AND SPECIALIST SERVICE
Obviously, your bike's brakes are among its most important safety related items. Do NOT dismantle or attempt to perform any work on the braking system unless you are fully competent to do so. If you have not been trained in this work, but wish to carry it out, we strongly recommend that you have a garage or qualified mechanic check your work before using the bike on the road. See also the section on BRAKES AND ASBESTOS in Chapter 1, Safety First for further information. Always start by washing the brakes with a proprietary brand of brake cleaner - wheels removed, where appropriate - never use compressed air to clean off brake dust. After fitting new brake shoes or pads, avoid heavy braking - except in an emergency - for the first 150 to 200 miles (250 to 300 km).

7A

7A. Raise the machine off the ground and check that both wheels revolve freely without the brakes binding. A small amount of movement should be possible in both the front brake lever and the rear brake pedal, before the brake begins to rub. Ideally, the front brake lever and the rear brake pedal should have about 1/4 in. movement before this begins to happen, but it is largely a question of individual preference. Make sure the front brake lever does not touch the handlebars before the brake is fully applied and that the rear brake can be fully applied with your foot still on the footrest.

7B. A front brake cable will have an adjuster at the brake drum end and perhaps an additional adjuster on the handlebar lever.

7C. The rear brake pedal will also have an adjuster of some kind at the brake drum end...

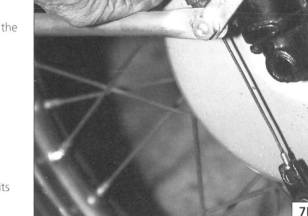

7B

7D. ...and usually has its own adjuster close to the footrest so that its height can be adjusted independently.

Some machines have alternative methods for taking up wear in brake shoes apart from cable or rod adjusters. For example, AJS and Matchless have thrust pins in the brake operating cam end of each brake shoe. They are a push fit in the end of the shoe and can be packed out by placing a washer beneath their underside.

7C

7D

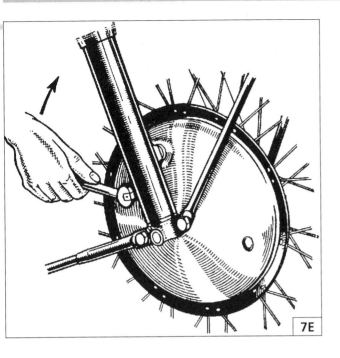

7E

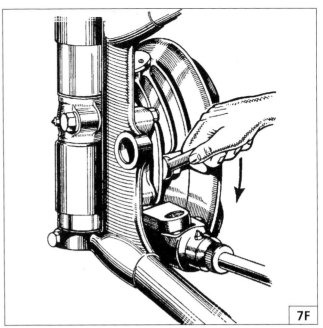

7F

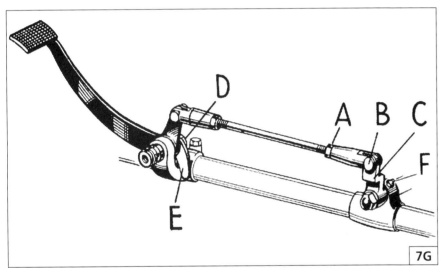

7G

7E. Ariel, the Sunbeam S7, and the S8 (rear brake only) models have an adjustable fulcrum screw in the brake plate, diametrically opposite the brake operating arm. In these latter cases, adjustment can be made from the outside, without having to remove the wheel to gain access to the brake shoes. This is the front adjuster...

7F. ...and this the rear on the Sunbeam S7 and S8.

7G. In cases where brake pedal height adjustment is available, do not use this adjustment to attempt to set the rear brake adjustment.

7H. Check that the rear brake stop light operates as soon as the brake pedal is depressed. Attention is usually necessary after the final drive chain tension has been adjusted. It can be made at the stop lamp switch either by adjusting the stretch of the pull-off spring, or by raising, lowering or tilting the switch itself.

7H

> **SAFETY FIRST!**
> **7I.** On drum brakes, the angle of the brake operating arm in its relaxed position is important, so that maximum leverage is applied when it is in the 'full on' position. There is always the danger of it going beyond the point of no return and causing the brake to lock on if all the adjustment has been taken up to compensate for badly worn brake linings. **THIS IS A VERY DANGEROUS SITUATION TO BE AVOIDED AT ALL COSTS.**
> Some brake operating arms are fitted on splines or a hexagon, so that their operating angle (and leverage) can be restored within reasonable limits. Note, however, that such a change does not compensate for badly worn linings and can also cause the brake to lock on in these circumstances, with dire consequences.

7I

TWIN LEADING SHOE BRAKES ONLY

7J. A twin leading shoe front brake as fitted to some high performance machines requires special attention if it is to be fully effective. Both brake shoes must contact the brake drum at exactly the same time. Most have two external operating arms joined together by an external, adjustable rod.

To check whether the brake is operating correctly, disconnect the linkage rod from one of the operating arms and apply both operating arms separately, noting the exact point at which the brake shoe first makes contact with the brake drum. Mark each operating arm and make a matching mark on the brake plate. Temporarily reconnect the linkage rod and adjust its length until the marks on the separate operating arms coincide exactly with their respective marks on the brake plate. Lock the adjustment and replace any split pins that had been removed from the linkage, using only new replacements.

Some twin leading shoe brakes do not have an external means of adjustment and only a general internal adjustment to take up brake lining wear. Adjustment is sometimes possible through an aperture in the rear of the brake drum, uncovered by prising out a rubber blanking plug.

DISC BRAKES ONLY

Disc brakes are self-compensating for wear and no adjustment is possible. Check that the brake pads have not worn down below

> **SAFETY FIRST!**
> **i)** If brake fluid should come into contact with the skin or eyes, rinse immediately with plenty of water. **ii)** It is acceptable for the brake fluid level to fall slightly during normal use, but if it falls significantly below the bottom of the filler cap neck, it indicates a leak or an internal seal failure. Stop using the bike and seek specialist advice immediately. **iii)** If you get dirt into the hydraulic system it can cause brake failure. Wipe the filler cap clean before removing. **iv)** You should only ever use only new brake fluid from an air-tight container. Old fluid absorbs moisture and this could cause the brakes to fail when carrying out an emergency stop or other heavy use of the brakes - just when you need them most and are least able to do anything about it, in fact!

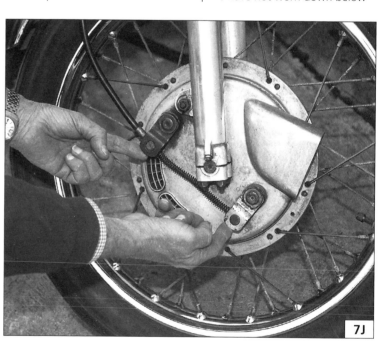

7J

their wear limit line, clearly marked around their edges. Check also that there are no signs of any brake fluid leakage from the hoses that carry the fluid or from the calipers that apply pressure to the pads. Make sure the brake fluid reservoir(s) is/are filled with brake fluid of the recommended specification.

8A

☐ Job 8. Checking the headlamp.

8A. Headlamp design changed during the period covered by this book. Initially, the most widely used units made by Lucas had a separate reflector and bulb holders with a rubber edge seal, attached by spring wire clips to the headlamp rim and glass. This arrangement was superseded by a sealed beam unit, in which the reflector and glass was a sealed unit clipped to the rim in similar fashion, with detachable bulb holders to facilitate bulb changes. Lucas units were by no means exclusive, however. A few manufacturers such as Velocette and Vincent preferred to fit equipment manufactured by H. Miller & Co., while a number of lightweight two-stroke manufacturers put their faith in units bearing the Wipac trademark.

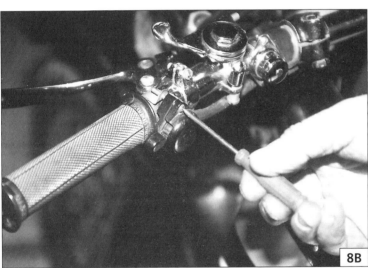

8B

8B. Check that the main headlamp bulb lights in both the main beam and dipped positions by operating the handlebar-mounted dip switch. If the bulb illuminates in only one position, make sure it is not the dipswitch that is at fault.

8C. Check by removing its cover and making sure the spring-loaded contact moves freely from one terminal to the other as the switch is operated. IMPORTANT NOTE: Two-strokes fitted with direct lighting need to have a special type of dipswitch in which a contact is not broken before the other is made. This prevents the bulb from blowing, as would occur due to a surge of current being created by the usual 'make and break' arrangement with its in-built pause.

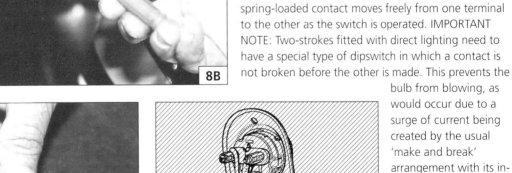

LIGHTING SWITCH

8C

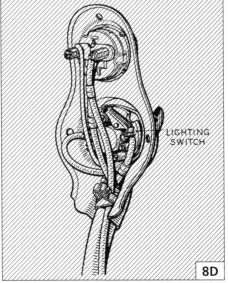

8D

8D. This is the panel containing switch (and ammeter), removed from the headlamp. (Illustration, courtesy Lucas)

500 MILE SERVICE

8E. If it appears the bulb is at fault, remove the headlamp rim from the headlamp. Usually it is retained by a catch at the bottom, or by a small screw through its top. In either case it will still be retained by a lip in the headlamp shell off which it will have to be lifted before it comes free. (Illustration, courtesy Lucas)

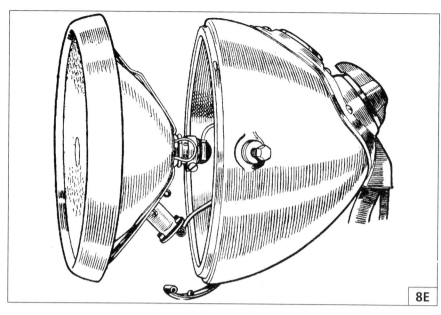

8E

8F. This is the Model F575P unit. (Illustration, courtesy Lucas)

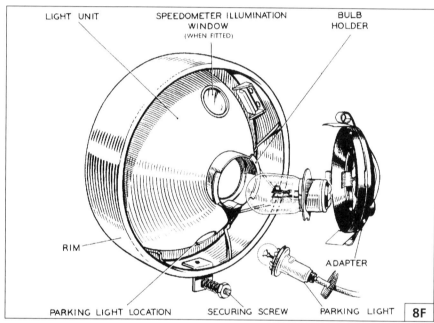

LIGHT UNIT   SPEEDOMETER ILLUMINATION WINDOW (WHEN FITTED)   BULB HOLDER

RIM

ADAPTER

PARKING LIGHT LOCATION   SECURING SCREW   PARKING LIGHT   8F

8G. A sealed beam unit uses a bulb with a flanged cap which will locate in only one position on the reflector. This ensures the main and dip filaments are correctly relocated and their focus setting retained. The bulb is held in position by a bayonet fixing cap that contains its contacts. Twist the cap anti-clockwise to free it and release the bulb. (Illustration, courtesy Lucas)

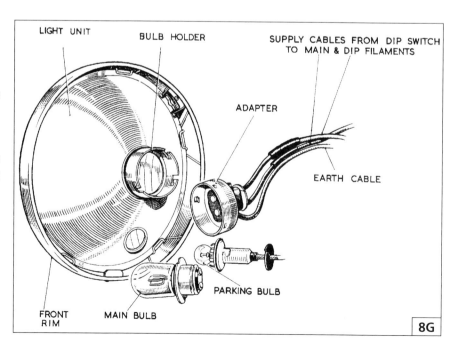

LIGHT UNIT   BULB HOLDER   SUPPLY CABLES FROM DIP SWITCH TO MAIN & DIP FILAMENTS

ADAPTER

EARTH CABLE

PARKING BULB

FRONT RIM   MAIN BULB   8G

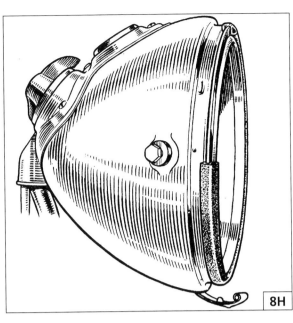

8H. Earlier headlamps will necessitate unclipping the reflector from the headlamp glass and rim, detaching the rubber sealing band, then removing the bulb from its holder which is part of the reflector. This bulb is of the bayonet fitting type and should be twisted to release it. Some headlamps have the main and pilot light bulbs in a separate bulb holder unit, retained in position by long wire clips. When unclipped, the holder with its bulbs will be free without need to disturb the reflector assembly. (Illustration, courtesy Lucas)

INSIDE INFORMATION: If the bulb will not free readily, or if the glass portion has worked loose in its cap, wrap it in rag so that if the glass breaks, it will not cut the fingers. If the bulb still refuses to free from its holder, separate the glass bulb from its cap by twisting it to and fro until its retaining wires break off and it will pull away. The cap can then be extracted by carefully bending part of it inwards while it is still held fast in the holder. Use a pair of snipe nosed pliers to twist it and lift it out of its holder.

8I. When replacing a bulb of the earlier type, note that its bayonet pins are offset, so that the bulb cannot be replaced upside down. Its cap will also be marked with the word 'TOP'. These precautions ensure the main and dip beam filaments remain in approximately their correct locations.

8J. Refocussing may be necessary after changing a bulb of this latter type. A clamp around the exterior of the bulb holder permits the bulb to be moved forward or backward after it has been slackened. Don't forget to retighten it after the correct bulb position has been found - see *Chapter 7, Getting Through the MOT.* (Illustration, courtesy Lucas)

8K. The pilot (parking) bulb is also usually contained within the headlamp shell and is easier to change. It too often has a push in and turn type of bayonet fixing in its bulb holder or it just pulls out of the headlamp back (see 8F). It may shine through a small window in a sealed beam unit, be underslung below the main headlamp shell or even in torpedo-shaped cases of its own, one on each side of the headlamp. Illustrated is the Lucas Model 550 parking light - unscrew the rim securing screw and peel back the rubber surround to release the lens. (Illustration, courtesy Lucas)

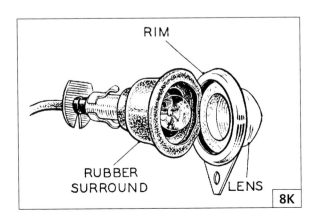

RIM

RUBBER SURROUND

LENS

Job 9. Check rear lights.

9A. The early rear lights were of what is known today as the 'fag end' type, which just about sums up the amount of light they put out! By modern standards they are totally inadequate, even when fitted with an obligatory 6 watt bulb.

9B. If a classic bike is used during the hours of darkness, riders are strongly recommended to fit a rear light of the more modern type with a wide plastic lens. Although it may detract from the bike's originality. It is far better to be seen from the rear, if only to forewarn the driver of the juggernaut bearing down on you!

9C. The acetate 'glass' frequently goes AWOL! Make up your own replacement from a piece of clear plastic from a plastic bottle.

IMPORTANT NOTE: Early rear lights may not have contained provision for a stop light originally, now a legal requirement that applies even if the machine is used only during daylight hours. They will have had to be modified to include this provision as it is also a requirement in the MOT Test that has to be fulfilled. If the rear light lens does not incorporate a reflector, one must be fitted separately.

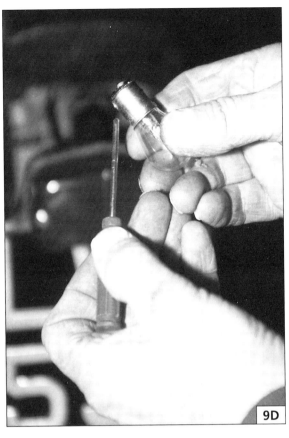

9D. A combined rear and stop light unit usually has one or two bulbs, both of which must be in working order. Separate bulbs will most likely be of the standard bayonet fitting type, whereas a combined rear and stop lamp bulb will have offset bayonet pins to prevent it being inserted upside down. Access in either case is by removing the plastic lens cover, or in older lights by unscrewing the bulb holder unit from the rear. Note the rear light must also illuminate the rear number plate.

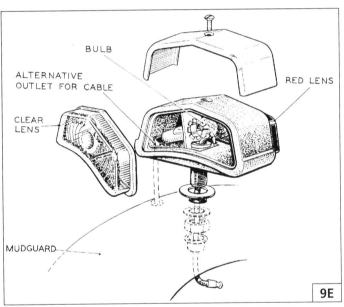

BULB

ALTERNATIVE
OUTLET FOR CABLE

RED LENS

CLEAR
LENS

MUDGUARD

9E. Apart from the obvious fixings shown in 9B, other lamp fixings include this sidecar lamp. (Illustration, courtesy Lucas)

9F. The 'fag end' type pushes in and is turned to the left. (Illustration, courtesy Lucas)

9G. On some models, the back of the lamp twists and removes. (Illustration, courtesy Lucas)

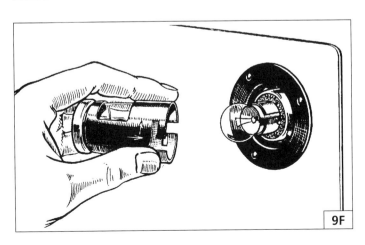

☐ Job 10. Check indicator lights.

10A. Only the more modern machines will be fitted with indicator lights. Problems usually arise from a faulty flasher unit, blown bulbs, or poor earth (ground) connections on the light units. If the lights operate on one side only, or flash at either a very high or low rate, the chances are that the flasher unit is defective. It is not repairable and will have to be renewed.

10B. A poor earth (ground) return may also create similar problems and will have to be checked out to find out whether a broken wire or a poor connection somewhere in the wiring system is responsible. This may require specialist attention if you are not familiar with wiring diagrams and the use of a multimeter when fault finding.

10A

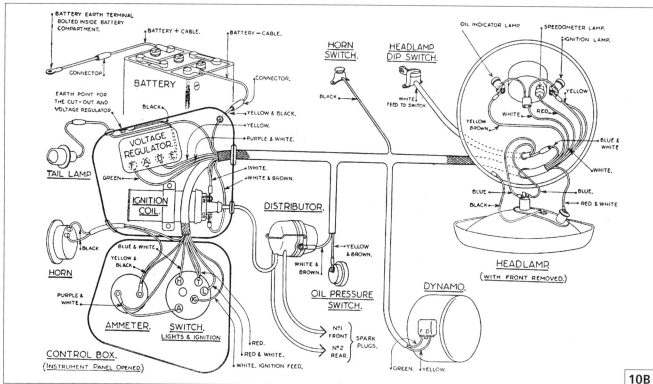

10B

Bulb changes are easy to make after removing the plastic lenses. They will be of the bayonet fixing type. Make sure you fit replacement bulbs of identical rating, otherwise the system will not function correctly.

10C. Handlebar switches do not often create problems unless they have been damaged in an accident or water has leaked in. Multi-function switches such as these (arrowed) are beyond repair by the average rider and will have to be renewed if defective.

10C

11A

Job 11. Using the grease gun.

The older the machine, the more grease nipples it is likely to have. Unless there is good reason otherwise, they require only two or three strokes of the gun.

> **SAFETY FIRST!**
> **In some instances over-greasing can prove dangerous. This applies in particular to wheel hubs, where grease can find its way on to the brake linings and impair their efficiency.**

Use a grease of the Castrol LM high melting point type unless otherwise specified. The places that require attention are:

11A. - the steering head bearings.

11B. - the wheel hubs which usually have to be part-dismantled and re-packed every 10,000 miles. (A few are fitted with a grease nipple.) (Illustration, courtesy Triumph)

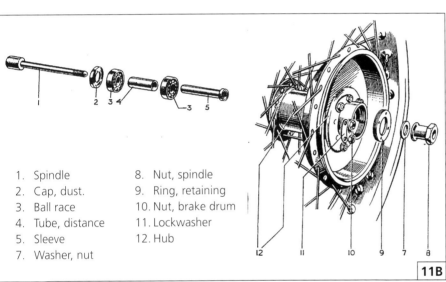

1. Spindle
2. Cap, dust.
3. Ball race
4. Tube, distance
5. Sleeve
7. Washer, nut
8. Nut, spindle
9. Ring, retaining
10. Nut, brake drum
11. Lockwasher
12. Hub

11B

11C. - the speedometer drive gearbox and the brake operating cam spindles, if a grease nipple is fitted.

11D. With a spring frame, the plunger or swinging arm suspension bearings will also require greasing in a similar manner.

11C

11D

11E. Some machines, like the early BSA singles, have oil holes instead of grease nipples on the brake operating cam spindle housings. Apply a light sewing machine type of oil to these and close the hole with the surrounding metal clamp provided.

11F. Particular attention is required to the post-war Douglas twins. Their torsion bar rear suspension relies on a system of bell crank levers to link the swinging arm with the torsion bars. Each bearing in this system has a grease nipple and will wear rapidly if grease is not applied frequently. Do not forget the main swinging arm bearings and also the grease nipple on the internal clutch operating arm. A notice about this is riveted to the small crankcase 'door' held by two nuts, behind which is the clutch operating mechanism on a Douglas.

11G. INSIDE INFORMATION: As many grease guns are made to fit the larger car-type grease nipples, it is often difficult to get a good enough seal between the grease gun and the smaller motorcycle-type nipple for the grease to be forced inside. This problem is easily overcome by placing a small piece of rag between the gun and the nipple. Invariably it will make an effective seal and ensure grease does not spill out around the outside of the nipple.

☐ Job 12. Clean the bike thoroughly.

It is unlikely that the owner of any classic bike will need to be reminded to clean it regularly. Almost without exception pride is taken in keeping a classic bike looking smart and tidy at all times, even to the extent of cleaning it down after every major run. Special care and attention is needed if the machine is used during the winter months, especially if there is snow and ice about, with salt spread on the roads. Under these circumstances, a thorough wash down is essential on return home, to offset the effects of corrosion that will already have started. The most vulnerable parts are those made in aluminium alloy, the wheel rims and other chromium plated parts, and the final drive chain. It may be necessary to remove the last mentioned from the machine and clean it thoroughly in a paraffin (kerosene) bath, before refitting it and re-lubricating it as described in Job 5.

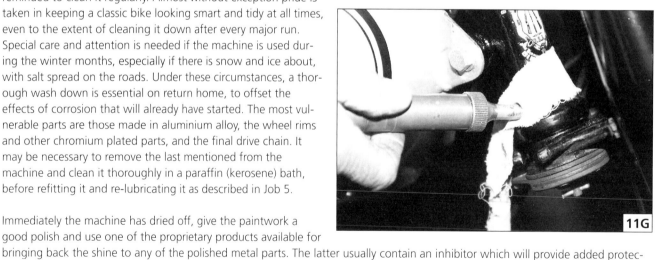

Immediately the machine has dried off, give the paintwork a good polish and use one of the proprietary products available for bringing back the shine to any of the polished metal parts. The latter usually contain an inhibitor which will provide added protection when the machine is next used under similar conditions.

This is also the time to touch up any damaged paintwork resulting from stone chips or scratches but do so before applying any polish to the affected areas. If you polish first, the paint will not stick. Another potential source of rusting is around any welded joint. Give the touch-up paint adequate time to dry and harden before polishing around the treated area.

1,500 miles - or Every Three Months, Whichever Comes First

OPTIONAL. First carry out Job 1 and omit Job 13, or Jobs 2 to 12. Preferably commence with Job 12, so that you start off with a clean bike, then:

Job 13. Change engine oil.

FOUR-STROKE ENGINES ONLY

OPTIONAL. Because today's fuels and lubricants are of much better quality than they were many years ago, engines tend to be much cleaner internally. As a result. oil changes need not be made as frequently as was originally recommended by the machine's manufacturer. However, there is still a tendency for owners of classic motorcycles to change the engine oil as originally intended, in the belief that the old adage 'oil is cheaper than bearings' still holds good.

In some respects there is some justification in this, as many of the older machines have only a somewhat crude oil filtration system, relying on metal gauze rather than the renewable felt elements or separate oil filter canisters that are commonplace today.

The older machines ran on a monograde oil, as today's multi-grade lubricants were at that time unknown. Generally speaking, it is believed that monograde oils are better suited to an engine with roller bearings as distinct from those of the shell type, even at the disadvantage of having to make seasonable oil changes to an oil of lower or higher viscosity in winter and summer respectively. Opinions vary widely, even among the oil manufacturers, so what type of oil to use and when to change it is, to a large extent, the machine user's decision. The only points to be borne in mind are that its viscosity should be that recommended by either the machine's manufacturer or the oil company, and that it should be changed according to their recommendations. In this latter respect, if the machine is used infrequently, for short journeys, in very dry and dusty conditions, or if it has been ridden hard for long periods, it is advisable to change the oil more frequently. For advice about changing the engine oil, refer to Job 18.

Two-strokes that have their own independent oil supply will not require an oil change because fresh oil is always being fed to the engine. While the decision about what type and viscosity of oil to use remains that of the user of the machine, it is worth noting that some oil companies market a specially formulated oil for two-stroke use. Self-mixing two-stroke oil should NEVER be used, however, except when the oil has to be mixed with the petrol (gasoline) in the fuel tank as the sole source of lubrication.

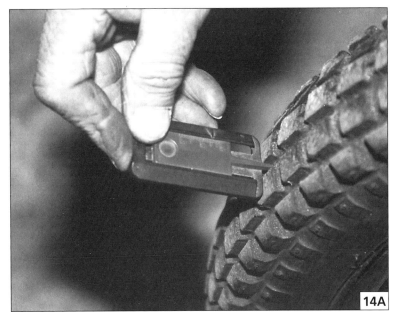

14A

Job 14. Check tyres condition.

14A. Check both tyres for tread depth, using a tread depth gauge. In the UK the minimum legal tread depth is 1.0mm over three quarters of the tread breadth around the tyre's entire circumference. Any motorcyclist is ill advised, however, to run a machine with the tread depth close to this limit. It is your life at stake as well as that of any other road users as even under the best of circumstances only a tiny portion of the tyre is in contact with the road surface. You need all the grip that you can get.

Check also for any damage to the sidewalls such as splits or cracks, or cracks around or in the tread pattern. If in any doubt renew the tyre. There is too much to be put at risk.

> **SAFETY FIRST!**
> *Tyres that show uneven wear tell their own story. If a tyre is worn more on one side than the other, the frame, forks or wheel are out of alignment and will require specialist attention to straighten them. If most wear has taken place in the centre, the chances are that the tyre is being run over-inflated. If the tread is worn more each side than at the centre, suspect under-inflation. Seek the advice of a tyre specialist, and also check that your tyre pressure gauge gives an accurate reading.*

Check also the tread of the tyre, removing any small stones or flints that have become embedded in the tread. If they are left in place they will gradually work their way into the tyre and eventually cause a puncture.

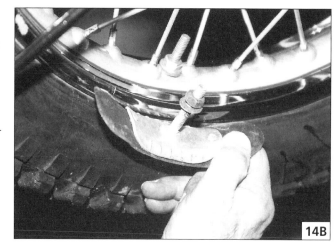
14B.

14B. Competition models are likely to have tyres fitted with at least one security bolt, to prevent the inner tube from creeping when the tyre is run at low pressure. Check that the security bolt nut is tight, otherwise the security bolt will not retain its grip on the inside wall of the tyre. Do not overtighten the nut, otherwise the leather or rubber washer beneath it, which keeps out water, may split.

IMPORTANT NOTE: See *Removing and Fitting Tyres* in *Chapter 7, Getting through the MOT*, if necessary.

☐ Job.15. Adjusting the sparking plug gap.

If the machine has more than one cylinder, number each of the sparking plug leads so that they are replaced in their original positions. Pull off the sparking plug cap(s) and unscrew the plug(s) from the cylinder head using the correct size socket or box spanner. Do this only after the engine has cooled down as otherwise the plug will be very hot and will burn your fingers. Take care not to drop it, or its ceramic insulator may be broken or damaged, or its gap closed up. Some specially-made plug spanners have an internal rubber insert which will grip the plug and hold it fast after it has been unscrewed.

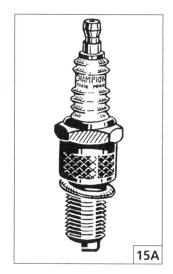
15A.

15A. Check each sparking plug to ensure it is in an acceptable condition by reference to the colour illustrations on page 65. Check also that the round terminal nut is tight, assuming the high tension lead is connected by means of a push-on cap. Clean the plug insulator as any accumulation of dirt or road debris may cause it to short out in wet weather or the high tension current to track down the insulator. This will result in a recurring misfire or even a complete ignition failure.

15B. Check the plug gap with a feeler gauge of the recommended thickness. A plug fitted to a machine with magneto ignition may have a gap within the range 0.018-0.022 in., or if it has coil ignition, 0.025-0.030 in. Check your machine's handbook. If necessary, adjust the gap so that the feeler gauge is a good sliding fit. To increase the gap, lever the side-mounted outer electrode outwards. To decrease the gap, tap the outer electrode on a hard surface. When the gap is set correctly, clean the electrode ends with a brass bristle wire brush.

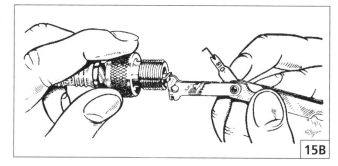
15B.

If either electrode is badly eroded or the inner or outer insulators damaged in any way, throw the plug away and fit a new replacement of identical grade. It is false economy to run with a damaged or badly worn plug. Make sure the plug grade follows the recommendation of the machine's manufacturer or that of the sparking plug manufacturer. If one of an incorrect grade is fitted it can cause engine damage, especially in a two-stroke engine.

Before refitting a plug, check that its threads are undamaged and smear them with graphite grease. This will make the plug easier to remove on future occasions and less likely to strip the thread in an aluminium alloy cylinder head. Make sure the thread engages correctly and the plug is not cross-threaded before tightening it. Use enough strength to ensure it seats firmly on its sealing washer but do not use excessive force which could result in a stripped cylinder head thread, particularly one cast in aluminium alloy.

☐ Job 16. Check HT lead(s)

16A. Make sure the high tension lead to each sparking plug is in good condition and free from any cracks or other forms of weathering.

INSIDE INFORMATION: If it is fitted with a protective cap where it connects with the sparking plug, unscrew the cap from the lead to check that water has not entered and is beginning to corrode away the inner wire. Make sure also that a protective rubber cap

16A.

fitted at the other end to prevent the entry of water into the magneto or coil connection. The cap at the sparking plug end should be either a tight fit around the HT lead, or be fitted with a clip that can be tightened to grip the lead firmly.

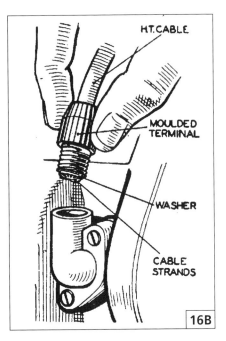

16B. If you need to renew the cable, don't forget to remove the brass washer from the old cable. Then, thread the knurled moulded nut over the lead, bare the end of cable for about 1/4 in., thread the wire through the metal washer and bend back the strands. Finally screw the nut into its terminal. (Please note that there are a number of variants of this type of fitting, which is for a Magdyno.) (Illustration, courtesy Lucas)

MULTI-CYLINDER ENGINES ONLY

16C. If the machine is one of the multi-cylinder type fitted with a distributor, remove the distributor cap and make sure it is free from cracks. Cracks will cause the HT current to track internally in damp or wet conditions. In such cases, replacement of the cap is the only satisfactory remedy.

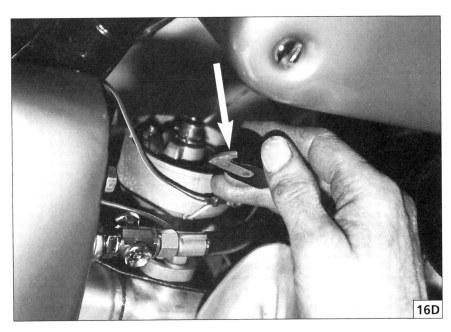

16D. Make sure the rotor arm shows no signs of burning (arrowed) and that the carbon brush that bears on it is not damaged or badly worn. Also, the shaft into which the rotor arm fits should be free from any excessive play, indicative of worn bearing bushes in the main body. Wear in this area will cause the contact breaker gap to vary constantly, so that it is no longer possible to set the ignition timing correctly. It may also leave a bright rub mark on the rotor arm. A distributor worn to this extent will have to be renewed as it is not feasible to remove the worn bushes and renew them.

1,500 MILE SERVICE

☐ Job 17. Contact breaker gap and magneto drive.

17A. The contact breaker gap is critical as the accuracy of the ignition timing is dependent on it. On machines fitted with a magneto it is usually 0.012 in. when the points are fully open, and on a coil ignition model 0.015 in. Check with the manufacturer's recommendations.

17B. Before checking the contact breaker gap, it is important to take a look at the condition of the points. If the machine has a coil ignition system, make sure the ignition is switched off first. If the points have a blackened and burnt appearance, this is a sure sign that the condenser in the ignition circuit has broken down and needs to be replaced.

SPECIALIST SERVICE. In a rotating armature magneto, this is a task beyond the average owner, as the magneto will have to be removed and completely dismantled to get at the condenser, which is part of the armature assembly. It will also necessitate fitting new contact breaker points as described in a later service interval check.

17C. If the points show no signs of burning or blackening, but have become badly eroded or worn, they will also have to be renewed. It is recommended the visual inspection is carried out first, as there is little purpose in checking (and perhaps resetting the gap) if it is later found that the points have to be renewed.

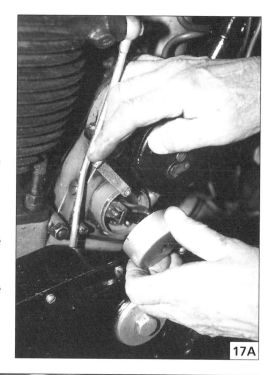
17A

17D. Two different types of contact breaker assembly are fitted to a rotating armature magneto: the face cam type used on most single cylinder models, or the circular cam ring type found on most twins. A Lucas Magdyno may have either type, depending on the type of machine to which it is fitted. In either case the non-adjustable point forms part of the moving arm that is operated by the cam. The adjustable point, immediately below the moving one, is threaded and can be raised or lowered, and locked in position by a lock nut.

IMPORTANT NOTE: AJS and Matchless fitted a Lucas SR1 rotating magneto in the mid-fifties, which was of the rotating magnet type. On this design the contact breaker remain stationary, the points being open and closed by a rotating cam. Adjustment is identical to that of a contact breaker in a coil ignition or distributor system.

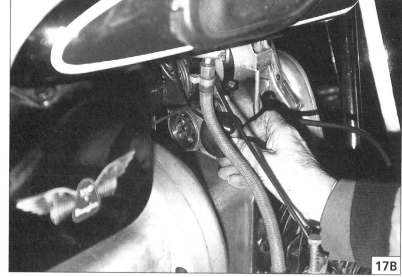
17B

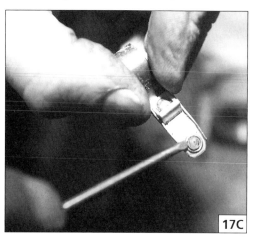
17C

17D

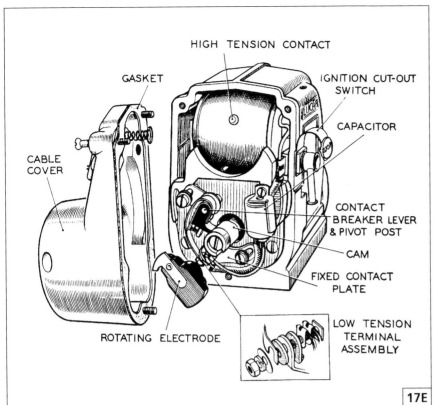

17E

HIGH TENSION CONTACT

GASKET

IGNITION CUT-OUT SWITCH

CAPACITOR

CABLE COVER

CONTACT BREAKER LEVER & PIVOT POST

CAM

FIXED CONTACT PLATE

ROTATING ELECTRODE

LOW TENSION TERMINAL ASSEMBLY

17E. Rotate the engine until the points are in their fully open position, with the push rod or heel that operates the moving point on the peak of the contact breaker cam. Take a feeler gauge of the correct thickness and raise or lower the adjustable point until the feeler is a good sliding fit in the gap between the points. Lock it in position with the lock nut. Remove the feeler gauge, rotate the engine until the points are fully open again and re-check the gap. (illustration, courtesy Lucas)

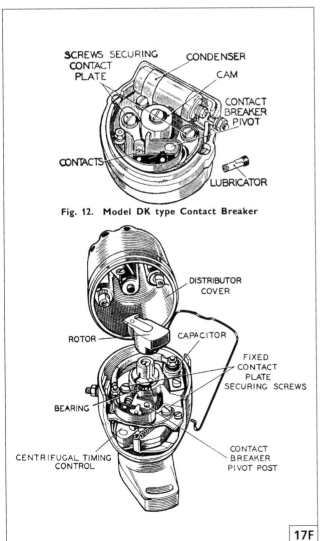

SCREWS SECURING CONTACT PLATE

CONDENSER

CAM

CONTACT BREAKER PIVOT

CONTACTS

LUBRICATOR

Fig. 12. Model DK type Contact Breaker

DISTRIBUTOR COVER

ROTOR

CAPACITOR

FIXED CONTACT PLATE SECURING SCREWS

BEARING

CENTRIFUGAL TIMING CONTROL

CONTACT BREAKER PIVOT POST

17F

17F. In coil ignition systems the contact breaker assembly is mounted on a circular baseplate that forms either part of the distributor assembly or is in a separate enclosure. The points are operated in a similar manner by a cam. As in the case of the magneto, one point is movable in relation to the other, usually by means of a screw in a slot. Slacken the screw to move the point inward or outward until the gap is correct when the points are fully open, then tighten the screw and re-check the gap is correct.

The contact breaker assembly fitted to many twin and to triple cylinder models has a separate set of contact points for each cylinder. This is an ideal situation as it is possible to adjust the points independently and set the ignition timing accurately for each cylinder. Some twin cylinder models have only one set of points that has to be shared by both cylinders. In theory this is acceptable, but only if the contact breaker cam has been machined accurately. Even a small error will mean only one cylinder can be timed accurately, leading to a compromise situation where the error will have to be shared between both cylinders to get them to run smoothly. **SPECIALIST SERVICE.** If the error is only small, this is no problem, but an error of any significance would take the edge off the machine's performance when it is shared between cylinders. Consult your specialist if necessary. (Illustration, courtesy Lucas)

17G. Most of the earlier two-strokes, especially those powered by a Villiers engine, have a flywheel magneto. On early models the contact breaker points are mounted on a baseplate inside the flywheel rotor so that access can be gained only through one of the apertures in the flywheel rotor. Later models have it within a separate enclosure. The correct contact breaker gap for a flywheel magneto assembly of this type is 0.012 to 0.015 in.

Irrespective of the type of contact breaker assembly, there are two areas which need to be lubricated very sparingly. Apply a couple of drops of oil to the pivot of the moving contact breaker point, and to the felt pad that lubricates the surface of the contact breaker cam. Do not exceed this amount, otherwise oil may get on to the contact breaker points and cause either a misfire or a complete ignition failure.

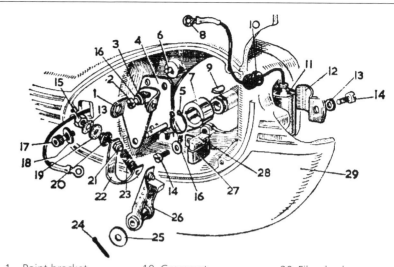

1. Point bracket	10. Grommet	20. Fibre bush
2. Fixing screw	11. Condenser	21. Point-bracket pin
3. Washer	12. Clip	22. Connecting strip
4. Base plate with pivot pin	13. Shakeproof washer	23. Rocker spring
5. Circlip	14. Screw	24. Split pin
6. Dowel	15. Nut	25. Washer
7. Contact-breaker cam	16. Washer	26. Rocker arm
8. Terminal	17. Screw	27. Oil-pad clip
9. Ignition-cam key	18. Washer	28. Oil pad
	19. Fibre Washer	29. Right-hand pad

17G

17H. Magnetos driven by chain need to have the chain tension checked regularly. If within a separate housing, first remove the outercover. Unscrew the bolt holding the gearchange lever in place...

17H

17I. ...and lift the lever away, pulling it off its shaft and allowing the chain cover to be accessed and removed.

INSIDE INFORMATION. It's all too easy to lose small screws, such as those holding the chain cover in place. Pop them into an old glass coffee jar for safe keeping. Replacement of even mundane Imperial-size fixings can sometimes be tricky - or inconvenient - to obtain.

17I

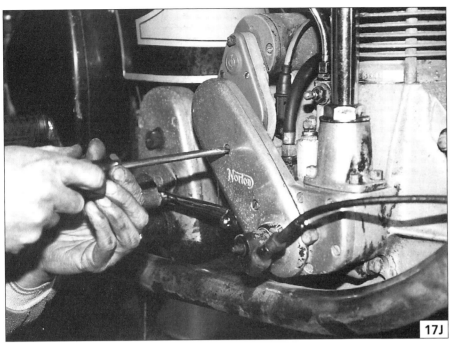

17J. Take out the screws holding the cover in place...

17K. ...and take off cover and tachometer drive, as a unit, where applicable.

17L. Freeplay in the chain should not exceed 3/4 in. up and down movement at its tightest spot, measured in the centre of its upper or lower run, to allow for engine expansion. Methods of adjustment vary, usually by either tilting the magneto mounting platform or by inserting packing pieces under the magneto base. Magnetos mounted endwise on the magneto chaincase have no means of adjustment. If the chain runs too slack under these circumstances it has to be renewed.

17M. Always re-check the tension after adjustment has been made. Grease the chain before replacing the cover.

3,000 Miles or Every Six Months, Whichever Comes First

First complete jobs 2 to 4, 6 to 12 and 14 to 17.

☐ **Job 18. Change the engine oil.**

> **SAFETY FIRST!**
> *Refer to the Section on ENGINE OILS in **Chapter 1, Safety First!** before carrying out the following work:*

Run the engine for a short while so that the oil gets warm, but not hot enough to scald. Run the engine in the open air or take the machine for a short run. DO NOT run the engine within a confined area as exhaust gases contain carbon monoxide which will kill without warning.

18A. With the machine on its stand or raised on a workbench, make sure it is held steady as recommended earlier. Place a container under the oil tank or crankcase compartment drain plug and after cleaning around the drain plug...

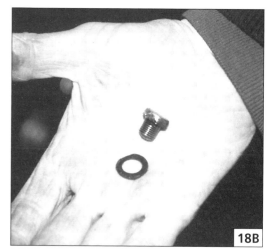

18B. ...unscrew it retaining the old fibre washer for now, in case of emergencies...

18C. ...and let the oil drain out. When all the oil has drained off completely...

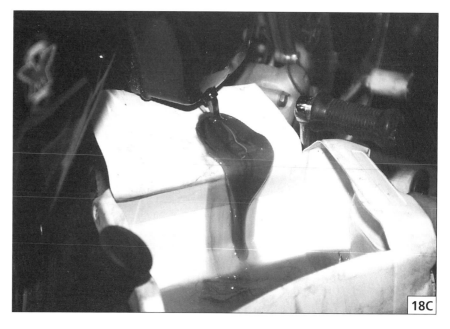

18D. ...replace and tighten the drain plug after fitting it with a new fibre washer.

SAFETY FIRST!
Drain plugs are notoriously tight, so make sure you use a socket or a ring of the correct size that will not slip, or take care when pushing on a screwdriver (as appropriate). The precautions already taken should ensure there is no possibility of the machine toppling over if force has to be used to unscrew the plug.

INSIDE INFORMATION: A metal gauze filter is usually fitted in the main outlet of the oil tank or compartment to screen out any debris in the oil before it reaches the oil pump. It should be removed and cleaned in paraffin (kerosene) before it is replaced. Note that some machines, such as BSA and Triumph, have an additional gauze filter retained by a metal plate and four nuts to the underside of the crankcase. After dismantling and cleaning the gauze, fit new gaskets in place of the originals to prevent future oil leaks. If the gauze is damaged, renew it.

If an oil tank or compartment contains any sludge, flush it out to remove it all before the filters are replaced and it is refilled. This task is easier with a separate oil tank, which can be removed first.

18E. Pour in fresh oil of the correct viscosity, taking care not to overfill the oil tank or compartment.

INSIDE INFORMATION: The level will drop on machines fitted with a separate oil filter chamber when the engine is run and this chamber fills up. Top up again to the correct level.

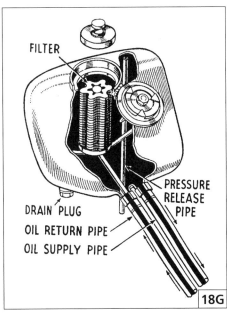

18F. Some machines, such as AJS, Matchless and Velocette, have a separate compartment within the oil tank containing a fabric oil filter element. It should be renewed at every other oil change; after covering only 3,000 miles cleaning it in a paraffin bath before replacing it should suffice, especially as some of these filter elements are now becoming difficult to obtain.

18G. This shows the location of the filter in a BSA oil tank.

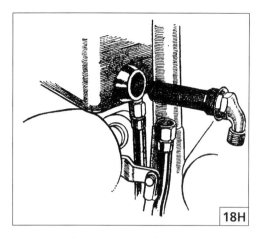

18H. Don't forget the mesh filter in the oil supply pipe on some models.

IMPORTANT NOTE: If the main oil outlet has a spring-loaded ball valve or similar anti-wet sumping device, THE PIPE MUST BE PRIMED WITH OIL BEFORE THE ENGINE IS STARTED. FAILURE TO DO SO WILL MEAN NO OIL IS DELIVERED TO THE OIL PUMP, WITH DISASTROUS CONSEQUENCES. Many of the Velocette singles have one of these ball valves fitted, and should have a warning notice on the oil tank to draw attention to the need for priming the main oil outlet pipe.

☐ Job 19. Lubricate dynamo, check the drive.

19A. A DC dynamo requires a small but regular amount of lubricant. A small aperture in the end cover is closed by a swivelling clip or a screw. Move the clip aside or unscrew the screw and add one or two drops of oil before closing the aperture. Lubricate sparingly as any excess oil may work its way on to the commutator and stop the dynamo charging.

19B. There may also be a removable grub screw at the driving end of the dynamo which should be unscrewed in a similar manner for lubrication. Pancake dynamos do not usually require lubrication.

19C. A few DC dynamos are belt driven, either by a flat or a 'V' belt. The former are more prone to slip if not adjusted correctly. The drive belt should be taut after adjustment, with no up or down play in the centre of its upper or lower run.

Separate chain driven dynamos will need to have the chain tension checked periodically. It should not have more than 1/4 in. up and down movement at its tightest spot measured in the middle of the upper or lower run. Adjustment can be made by slackening the clamp around the dynamo and turning the dynamo in the appropriate direction before re-tightening the clamp. Always re-check the chain's tension after making such an adjustment. AC (alternator) electrics require no attention other than a periodic check of the wiring and its connectors.

20A

20B

☐ Job 20. Adjust carburettor/s.

OPTIONAL: If necessary, to adjust carburettor/s, see Job 45.

TWIN-CARBURETTOR MODELS ONLY
Some twin cylinder machines are fitted with twin carburettors. It is important that both are completely in step with each other, otherwise the engine will run unevenly and not respond to the throttle as well as it might. Unfortunately, they do have a tendency to drift out of harmony from time to time, and require re-setting to correct this.

If the fault has suddenly occurred, first make sure it cannot be attributed to anything else. DO NOT ALTER THE SETTING OF EITHER CARBURETTOR UNTIL YOU HAVE MADE SURE THEY OPEN AND CLOSE AT EXACTLY THE SAME TIME.

20A. Some machines have twin throttle cables, each with its own adjuster, so it is easy to make whatever adjustments are necessary to ensure both throttle slides open and close at the same time. It is unlikely the position of either throttle stop screw will need to be altered, unless one has worked slack. Where a single cable is used, which splits into two cables at a junction box, individual adjustment will have to be made by the threaded adjuster on each carburettor top.

20B. INSIDE INFORMATION: A simple dodge to check whether the carburettor slides begin to lift at exactly the same time is to place a lollipop stick under each, trapped by the inner facing edge of the slide. As soon as the slide begins to lift, the grip on the lollipop stick will be released and it will tilt downward. This is especially useful on a Douglas, where the carburettors are far apart. Obviously this check has to be made with the engine not running. Make sure there is no chance of either lollipop stick disappearing down the inlet port!

☐ Job 21. Check air filter.

21A. To begin with, British motorcycle manufacturers were remarkably complacent about the need to fit an air filter, so that most of the early post-war models have none. However, as the export market began to grow, and there was an increasing need for them to be fitted, they became available either as a standard fitting or as an optional extra. (This is the common 'D'-shaped type. The Villiers version is a round-shaped alternative to the same thing.)

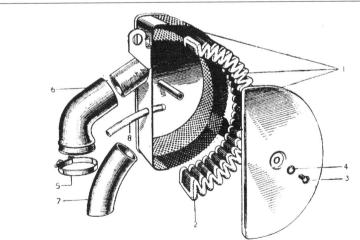

1. Filter assembly
2. Filter element
3. Cover screw
4. Shakeproof washer
5. Clip connexion to carburettor
6. Connexion, Amal carburettor to filter (rubber)
7. Connexion, S.U. carburettor to filter (rubber)
8. Vent pipe, carburettor to filter

21A

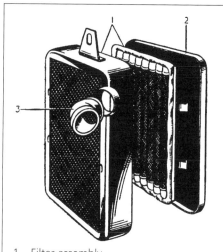

1. Filter assembly
2. Element with cover
3. Connexion sleeve (rubber)

21B

21B. Other types have a disposable pleated paper element. In either case they require regular attention, otherwise petrol consumption will rise and performance fall off as they become blocked. This woven felt type, from a Triumph, has an oil soaked element.

21C. Filters with a felt or a foam element need to have the filter unit removed so that access can be gained to the element which may, or may not, be attached to the cover. Clean the element thoroughly in a bath of paraffin (kerosene). Allow it to drain off and dry then lightly oil it with SAE 20 oil or whatever is recommended by the manufacturer. Do not soak it heavily and allow any excess oil to drain off before reassembling the filter unit and replacing it on the machine. If the element is one of the sponge or foam type, it can be wrung out to remove any excess oil, provided its structure is not damaged. An old and a new foam filter are shown in the accompanying photograph.

21C

Filters containing a paper element require the old element to be discarded and a new replacement fitted. If a new replacement is not available, it can be re-used (unless it is well clogged!) after it has been blown clear by compressed air, applying pressure from the INSIDE. A paper element that is wet or covered in oil or any other fluid is NOT suitable for re-use.

21D. When re-connecting the filter unit to the carburettor(s), make sure the connecting hose is not split, trapped, or damaged in any way. **SPECIALIST SERVICE.** If it is necessary to run without the air filter connected (but note that engine life will be reduced if you do so), increase the size of the carburettor's main jet. **FAILURE TO CHANGE THE MAIN JET SIZE WILL RESULT IN ENGINE DAMAGE.** When an air filter is fitted, a smaller main jet is fitted to the carburettor to compensate for the richening up of the mixture by the restriction of the air inlet.

21D

Job 22. Change primary chaincase oil.

22. The oil in the primary chaincase needs changing frequently as it suffers from condensation. Drain off all the old oil by removing the chaincase drain plug. Replace the drain plug with a new fibre washer and refill the chaincase with the recommended quantity and viscosity of oil.

Job 23. Final drive chain lubrication and alteration.

23A. INSIDE INFORMATION: To lubricate the final drive chain more thoroughly than is possible with a spray-on aerosol, remove the spring link that joins both ends and take the chain off the machine. Removal (and refitting) is made much easier if a length of old chain is connected to it and drawn on in its place. The chain can then be disconnected after the old chain is wrapped around the usually inaccessible gearbox sprocket, reconnected and drawn back again into position after it has been lubricated.

23B. After removal, wash the chain thoroughly in a paraffin (kerosene) bath, a messy task where disposable gloves are invaluable, then dry it off with some clean rag.

SAFETY FIRST!
Chain grease is usually supplied in circular tins which conveniently can also be used as the bath in which to immerse the chain once the grease has been heated sufficiently to make it molten. DO NOT OVERHEAT AS THE GREASE IS NOT ONLY HIGHLY FLAMMABLE BUT WILL ALSO CAUSE VERY SERIOUS BURNS IF SPILT ON THE SKIN. ONLY CARRY OUT THIS JOB OUT OF DOORS ON A NON-FLAMMABLE SURFACE. ALSO BE AWARE THE BATH WILL TILT VERY EASILY IF IT IS RAISED WHILE ITS CONTENT IS STILL MOLTEN OR AS THE CHAIN IS BEING RAISED OR LOWERED. ALLOW THE GREASE TO COOL AND SOLIDIFY BEFORE LIFTING IT FROM ITS HEAT SOURCE. DO NOT HEAT IT OVER A NAKED FLAME. ALWAYS WEAR OVERALLS, SLEEVES BUTTON DOWN, HEAVY-DUTY GLOVES AND GOGGLES.

23C. Attach a piece of wire firmly to one end, then immerse it completely in a bath of molten chain grease.
Leave it immersed while the grease is kept molten, then, AFTER TURNING OFF THE HEAT AND PLACING THE GREASE BATH ON A STABLE, HEAT-PROOF SURFACE, withdraw the chain by holding the wire attachment and using it to suspend the chain vertically so that the molten grease can drain into the grease bath. The chain will be very hot, so take care not to get burnt by either the chain or the molten grease. Allow the grease to solidify and the chain to cool completely before putting it back on the machine.

INSIDE INFORMATION: This is definitely NOT a job to be carried out in a kitchen on a cooker. Removing solidified graphite grease from floor tiles or linoleum is no mean task, to say nothing of how it will impair even the best of domestic relationships!

CHAIN ALTERATIONS AND REPAIRS

IMPORTANT NOTE: Broadly speaking, this practice held good until about the mid-1950s. As engine power began to increase significantly, and unit-construction engines came into use, the connecting link was no longer considered safe. If anything happened and the chain broke, it would bunch up in the chaincase, smash it, and quite possibly lock the engine solid. Some even used this as a method of shortening a chain when it became badly stretched, an even worse situation. Almost everyone overlooked the fact that when a chain was re-riveted you needed a joining link that had pins with softened ends so that they could be peened over.

23C

We suggest this technique holds good only for early post-war bikes, otherwise an endless chain is the only answer. Note, it is very bad practice indeed to use two spring links in close proximity to each other, as in 23I.

23D

23D. To shorten a chain containing an even number of pitches remove the dark parts shown...

23E

23E. ...and replace by cranked double link and single connecting link.

23F. To shorten a chain containing an odd number of pitches remove the dark parts shown...

23F

23G. ...and replace by single connecting link and inner link.

23H. To repair a chain with a broken roller or inside link remove the dark parts shown...

23I. ...and replace by two single connecting links and one inner link.

INSIDE INFORMATION: This must only be considered as a very temporary, emergency measure, since it is very bad practice to run a machine with a chain with two (or worse still, more!) joining links.

23J. INSIDE INFORMATION: Refitting the spring link is made easier if the ends of the chain are pressed into the teeth of the rear wheel sprocket.

23K. Make sure the spring link, is fitted correctly, with its closed end facing the direction of the chain's travel.

*23L. INSIDE INFORMATION: Use of the old-style rivet extractors - the sort of thing you may pick up at an autojumble - is no longer considered to be good practice. Special joining links with soft-headed pins are no longer available. If a chain is worn, renew both it **and** the sprockets.*

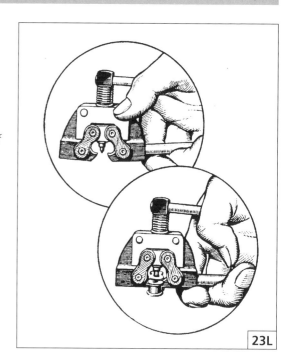

23L

☐ Job 24. Check and lubricate cables and rods.

Control cables lead a hard life, being exposed to the elements at all times. It is wise to check that their outer covering has not split or is trapped or damaged in any way, otherwise water can enter and eventually cause the inner wire to rust and seize up. If in any doubt, renew the cable.

24A. Check to ensure the inner cable has no broken strands and that the nipple is not in danger of pulling off either end. Renewal of the cable will be necessary if either of these faults are found.

Each cable should operate smoothly and without any jerkiness. Proprietary cable lubricators are available which permit a cable to be lubricated while it is still in position. Alternatively, the uppermost end can be disconnected from its control and a funnel made of plasticene or some similar material into which the lubricating oil can be poured. Keep the cable vertical and allow the oil to work through to the cable's furthest end before re-connecting it.

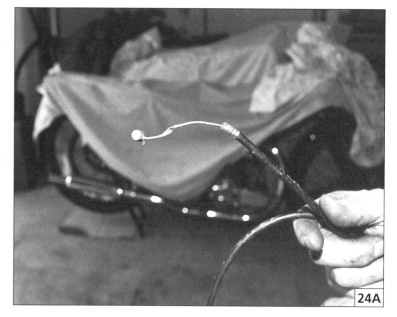

24A

24B. Many rear brakes are rod-operated. Lightly oil or grease the clevis pins (arrowed) in the joints and check that each is secured by a split pin. If the rear brake pedal or the rear brake operating arm is fitted with a return spring, that can be checked at the same time. This also applies to the front brake.

24B

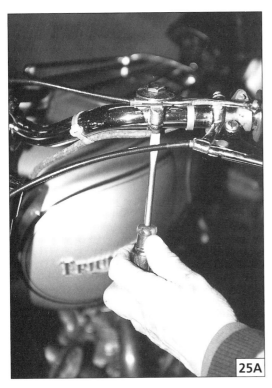

25A

Job 25. Check handlebar-mounted controls.

25A. The handlebar controls should be checked to ensure their mountings are tight and that they have a firm grip on the handlebars. They should also operate smoothly.

25B. Make sure their pivots are kept well lubricated; if necessary the ignition advance and air levers can be dismantled for internal greasing.

25C. The twist grip throttle and ignition advance and air levers have provision for adjustment so that they will remain in one set position. The twist grip has a small set screw on its underside, held fast by a lock nut. It bears on an internal friction damper and can be adjusted to prevent the twist grip from closing immediately the hand is taken off it. Tightening the centre screw or nut will have a similar effect on the ignition and air control levers.

25B

25D. The rubber grips fitted to the twist grip and the bare left-hand end of the handlebars tend to work loose after extended usage. This can make it difficult to operate the twist grip. Water can also creep under them, to make the situation even worse. If the dummy grip on the left-hand end of the handlebars comes off as the machine is being raised on to its stand, it can easily topple over. The only remedy is to fit new grips and if necessary, to dry the handlebars and coat them with an impact adhesive before the grips are slid into position.

25C

25D

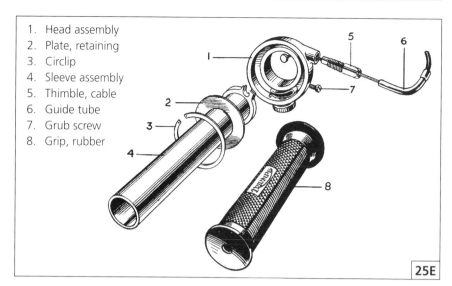

1. Head assembly
2. Plate, retaining
3. Circlip
4. Sleeve assembly
5. Thimble, cable
6. Guide tube
7. Grub screw
8. Grip, rubber

25E. Typical Triumph twist grip components when broken down. (Illustration, courtesy Triumph)

Job 26. Check wheels.

26A. The wheels fitted to the machines covered by this book are of the wire spoked variety. Check each individual spoke on both wheels to make sure none are broken, bent (arrowed), or beginning to work loose.

26B. In the latter case, a quick check can be made by tapping them with a spanner or some similar object, when each spoke should give a similar 'ring'. A loose spoke will be immediately obvious.

26C. If a loose spoke requires only minor tightening of its nipple, this is acceptable, provided it does not begin to pull the wheel out of line. Otherwise, it will be necessary to remove the wheel from the machine, and its tyre and inner tube. The spoke ends are ground off where they extend from the nipple inside the wheel rim, otherwise they will dig into the inner tube and eventually cause a puncture. **SPE-CIALIST SERVICE.** When several loose spokes are found, or if any are broken, this becomes a job for the experienced wheel builder, to ensure the rim is kept true to the wheel hub.

26D. INSIDE INFORMATION: A properly built wheel should not have any exposed spoke threads on this part of the spoke. If it does, it's a **SPECIAL-IST SERVICE** *job: have a specialist put things right for you.*

6,000 Miles - or Every Twelve Months, Whichever Comes First

First complete jobs 2 to 12 and 14 to 26, then:

☐ **Job 27. Check brake shoes or pads.**

DRUM BRAKES ONLY

SAFETY FIRST! AND SPECIALIST SERVICE
*Obviously, your bike's brakes are among its most important safety related items. Do NOT dismantle or attempt to perform any work on the braking system unless you are fully competent to do so. If you have not been trained in this work, but wish to carry it out, we strongly recommend that you have a garage or qualified mechanic check your work before using the bike on the road. See also the section on BRAKES AND ASBESTOS in **Chapter 1, Safety First!** for further information. Always start by washing the brakes with a proprietary brand of brake cleaner - wheels removed, where appropriate - never use compressed air to clean off brake dust. After fitting new brake shoes or pads, avoid heavy braking - except in an emergency - for the first 150 to 200 miles (250 to 300 km).*

27A. Note the 'shadow' area on this drawing. When the brake lever is in this position with the brake off, you've got strong evidence that the linings are **badly** worn. However, as there is no other external wear indicator, the wheels should be removed as shown below to check the condition of the brake shoe linings. (Illustration, courtesy Triumph)

SAFETY FIRST!
Make sure the machine is firmly supported by more than its centre or rear stand alone before removing the wheels.

27B. In many cases, the front or rear mudguard will have to be removed too, disconnecting rear lamp wiring, as necessary. (Illustration, courtesy Triumph)

27C. Remove the rear chain and the torque arm (arrowed), if fitted. Also, disconnect the speedometer cable, on those models where the drive is off the hub.

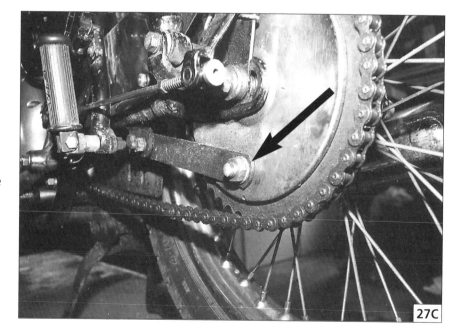

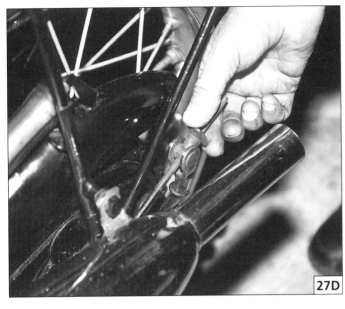

27D. Remove the brake rod adjuster nut, when rod operated brakes are fitted.

27E. When cable-operated brakes are fitted, take out the split pin and detach the clevis pin and cable.

27F. After slackening the spindle nuts, the wheel can be withdrawn and the spindle removed. Take note of the correct order and position of every single shim and washer.

27G. The brake assembly simply lifts away from the hub.

27H. You can now check the condition of the linings. Where the brake shoes have riveted on linings, once common practice, it is important that the point has not been reached where the rivet heads are about to contact the brake drum's surface. If they do, they will score it badly and reduce braking efficiency. It may still be possible to find replacement linings that can be riveted on in their place, otherwise bonded-on linings are the only alternative.

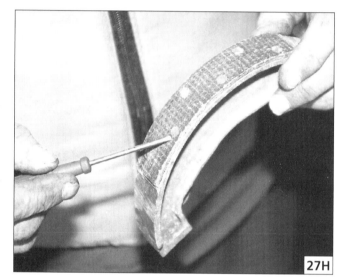

27I. If bonded-on linings are already fitted, the thickness of lining remaining will be the best guide. If it is half way below its original thickness and/or the brake operating arm has lost most of its leverage, the shoes need to be renewed. Check also that each lining is bonded firmly to the shoe and has not broken away at any point. Bonded-on linings have been known to detach themselves completely from a shoe as the result of a poor initial bond, often difficult to detect. If they do so, a serious accident can result from a locked wheel.

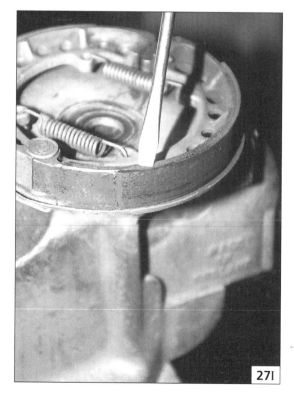

You can learn a lot about the condition of an engine from looking at the spark plugs. The following information and photographs, reproduced here with grateful thanks to NGK, show you what to look out for.

1. Good Condition
If the firing end of a spark plug is brown or light grey, the condition can be judged to be good and the spark plug is functioning at its best.

4. Overheating
When having been overheated, the insulator tip can become glazed or glossy, and deposits which have accumulated on the insulator tip may have melted. Sometimes these deposits have blistered on the insulator's tip.

6. Abnormal Wear
Abnormal electrode erosion is caused by the effects of corrosion, oxidation, reaction with lead, all resulting in abnormal gap growth.

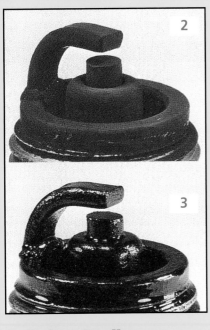

5. Normal Wear
A worn spark plug not only wastes fuel but also strains the whole ignition system because the expanded gap requires higher voltage. As a result, a worn spark plug will result in damage to the engine itself, and will also increase air pollution. The normal rate of gap growth is usually around 'half-a-thou.' or 0.0006 in. every 5,000 miles (0.01 mm. every 5,000 km.).

7. Breakage
Insulator damage is self-evident and can be caused by rapid heating or cooling of the plug whilst out of the car or by clumsy use of gap setting tools. Burned away electrodes are indicative of an ignition system that is grossly out of adjustment. Do not use the car until this has been put right.

2. Carbon Fouling
Black, dry, sooty deposits, which will eventually cause misfiring and can be caused by an over-rich fuel mixture. Check all carburettor settings, choke operation and air filter cleanliness. Clean plugs vigorously with a brass bristled wire brush.

3. Oil Fouling
Oily, wet-looking deposits. This is particularly prone to causing poor starting and even misfiring. Caused by a severely worn engine but do not confuse with wet plugs removed from the engine when it won't start. If the "wetness" evaporates away, it's not oil fouling.

6,000 MILE SERVICE

27J. Brake shoes are removed easily by levering up one of the shoes, taking the tension off the two springs and taking the assembly off the backplate.

INSIDE INFORMATION: Brake shoe removal and replacement is made easy if the brake shoes with their springs attached are prised away from the brake operating cam and expanded to their fullest amount, then raised upward together in the form of a 'V' and lifted off.

27J

LUBRICATE BRAKE OPERATING CAM

27K. At this stage, the brake operating cam should be serviced - it often isn't! With the brake backplate gripped - but protected against marking - in the vice, it is *essential* to mark the position of the brake lever on its spindle by scribing a mark, before unbolting and removing the lever.

27K

27L. Actually, on a square shaft, you can't go far wrong, but if it's splined, and you lose the correct position, it can be a nuisance to re-establish it.

27L

27M. Unscrew the nut holding the cam into the backplate until it is flush with the end of the spindle, then tap it free with a soft-faced mallet. (If it's this tight, it needs lubrication!)

27N. Clean off, lubricate with fresh LM (high melting point) grease...

27O. ...and refit to the backplate.

27P

27Q

27P. Refitting the shoes goes: springs first; clip shoes back down and into place (*without* trapping fingers!) ...

27Q. ...ensuring that the shoe ends are located properly on the abutment plate and the operating cam. **IMPORTANT NOTE.** As you can see from this demonstration carried out partly on an old BSA Bantam unit, your hands will become dirtier and greasier as the work progresses. Wash them before fitting new brake shoes.

INSIDE INFORMATION: Cover the friction surfaces of all new brake shoes with masking tape until the job is complete, so ensuring that they are kept free of dirt or grease. Don't forget to remove the masking tape! Write a note on each piece of tape as a visual reminder.

27R. SAFETY FIRST!
Always fit new split pins and tab washers when reassembling,
wherever they are used.

27R

27S. IMPORTANT NOTE: Be sure to locate the brake backplate when reassembling, either by locating the stud (A) on the brake anchor plate in the fork channel (B), or by refitting the torque arm illustrated in 27C. (Illustration, courtesy Triumph)

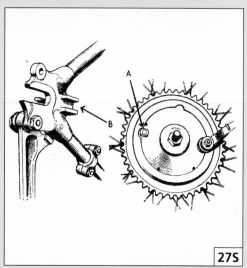

27S

DISC BRAKES ONLY

SAFETY FIRST! AND SPECIALIST SERVICE
i) Obviously, your bike's brakes are among its most important safety related items. Do NOT dismantle or attempt to perform any work on the braking system unless you are fully competent to do so. If you have not been trained in this work, but wish to carry it out, we strongly recommend that you have a garage or qualified mechanic check your work before using the bike on the road. See also the section on BRAKES AND ASBESTOS in Chapter 1, Safety First! for further information. ii) Always start by washing the brakes with a proprietary brand of brake cleaner - wheels removed, where appropriate - never use compressed air to clean off brake dust. iii) After fitting new brake shoes or pads, avoid heavy braking - except in an emergency - for the first 150 to 200 miles (250 to 300 km). iv) If brake fluid should come into contact with the skin or eyes, rinse immediately with plenty of water. v) It is acceptable for the brake fluid level to fall slightly during normal use, but if it falls significantly below the bottom of the filler cap neck, it indicates a leak or an internal seal failure. Stop using the bike and seek specialist advice immediately. vi) If you get dirt into the hydraulic system it can cause brake failure. Wipe the filler cap clean before removing. vii) You should only ever use only new brake fluid from an air-tight container.

27T. As mentioned previously, disc brake pads can be checked while they are still in position, the wear limit being marked very clearly on their edges. It is preferable to renew the pads when there is still 1/16 in. to go before the wear limit is reached, as a safety factor.

27U. If you have sufficient experience and confidence to remove and renew the brake pads yourself, start by straightening the ends of the two split pins that retain them in place...

27V. ...and pull them out, freeing the brake pads.

27W. If the pads are tight, as is quite probable, use a pair of long nose pliers to press the pads sideways toward the body of the brake caliper and free them, or push with a screwdriver, but *don't* twist against the disc - damage could cause brake failure!

27X. The old pads can now be withdrawn, tugging with pliers or self-grip wrench, as necessary.

27Y. The new pads will probably prove impossible to fit until you push back the piston(s) that bear on them into the brake caliper levering them back in with a piece of wood or tightening a clamp taking great care not to damage pistons or seals. In doing so, this will cause the brake fluid level in the reservoir to rise, so take precautions to ensure any overflow does not damage the paintwork or any plastic components in its vicinity. It is advisable to clean very carefully the inside of the caliper before the new pads are fitted, removing any dirt or rust from the exposed areas of the piston(s). Take great care the piston(s) do not move outward as if they come out of their housing(s) brake fluid will be lost and the system will have to be bled to free it of any air that may have entered.

27W

27X

SAFETY FIRST! and SPECIALIST SERVICE.
*Do not use an abrasive of any kind to clean the piston(s). If they are badly corroded or stuck fast, specialist attention will be required necessitating draining the hydraulic system and removing the complete caliper unit. Otherwise, apply a **very** light coating of brake grease around the piston(s), often supplied with the new pads or obtainable separately from whoever supplied the pads. Apply sparingly - grease on the pads could, literally, be fatal!*

27Y

Slide in the new pads after smearing the back of their metal back plate with a very small amount of special brake grease, not ordinary grease. Avoid getting any on the pad surfaces. Refit any springs that prevent brake pad rattle and brake squeal, and retain the assembly with new split pins. Don't forget to spread the ends of each pin so that they cannot work their way out.

27Z.

SAFETY FIRST!
When cleaning brake drums, shoes and disc brake components, take great care not to inhale the dust. Older brake shoes and pads contained asbestos, which is very toxic if breathed in and can cause lung cancer.
Note that irrespective of whether new brake shoe linings or pads are fitted, time will be needed for them to bed in correctly. They can also glaze over if the brakes are applied very hard during their 'running in' period. It takes about 150 to 200 miles for new linings or pads to gain their full operating efficiency, so until this has been achieved the stopping distance will be increased. It may take an even greater number of miles if the brake drum or disc is scored as the linings or pads will have to assume their profile before working effectively.

27Z. Check the discs for scoring. Light scoring may be faced off by an engineering shop but if scoring is too deep, or if the disc is cracked, you must replace with new. **SPECIALIST SERVICE**. If you're unsure, seek specialist advice - you're life could depend on it!

☐ Job 28. Check seating.

28A. The earlier models covered by this book will be fitted with a single saddle and a pillion seat. A saddle rarely requires any attention, other than regular greasing of the pivot bolt that serves as its front mounting point. Some machines are fitted with a grease nipple at this point to save having to remove the bolt for greasing. The saddle cover is attached by clips and is easily replaced when it becomes worn.

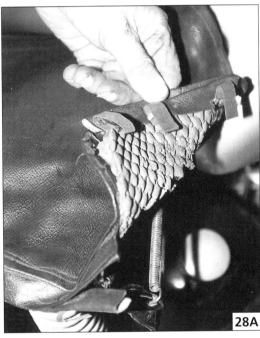

28A.

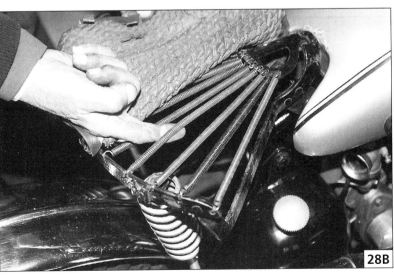

28B.

28B. The mattress-type springs across the frame below the cover can also be easily replaced if any of them break. Note they are of differing lengths and sometimes there may be aeroelastic in their place.

28C. Pillion seats come in a variety of different forms, some better sprung than others. Most manufacturers fitted a rexine-covered sponge rubber slab as standard. Often referred to as an upholstered brick, this apt description sums up their comfort factor! Securely mounted pillion footrests are a legal requirement.

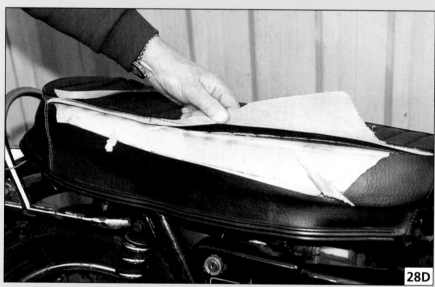

28D. Dual seats came into fashion during the early fifties, when rear suspension came into fashion. The cover, and particularly its stitches, tend to disintegrate due to the combined effects of wear and weather. Elasticated replacement covers that fit over the top of the original are available and there is also a proprietary seat recovering service - see adverts in classic bike magazines.

The metal base of a dual seat rarely receives attention as it is hidden out of sight. Long term, it is likely to rust or split, and collapse, necessitating replacement of the seat. Some replica dual seats now have a fibreglass base for this reason.

☐ **Job 29. Instruments.**

29A. A motorcycle has very few instruments, usually a speedometer and an ammeter. Some, such as the early Norton and Triumph twins and some Ariels, may also have an oil pressure gauge fitted in the petrol tank top instument panel.

It is a legal requirement for the speedometer to be in good working order and to provide an accurate reading. Usually attached to the handlebars or enclosed within the headlamp shell or a nacelle, it can also be found sunk into the top of the petrol tank on early post-war BSAs. Some sporting machines have a matching tachometer to record the engine speed in rpm.

29B. Internal illumination in a speedometer is provided by a low wattage bulb. The bulbholder is of the bayonet type, retained by a threaded ring in the bottom of the speedometer casing. It requires a special small size head bulb.

29B

29C. The ammeter is usually mounted in the headlamp shell and may be part of a detachable housing that contains also the headlamp switch (see illustration 8D). It may also be found in a headlamp nacelle or sometimes mounted in an enclosure below the seat that contains also the ignition switch. It is not internally illuminated but some ammeters such as those of Miller manufacture have a 'window' cut in their base through which reflected light from the headlamp can shine.

The ammeter gives a visual indication of whether the dynamo or alternator is charging the battery. It should show a discharge reading when the engine is stopped and the lights are switched on, but it should register a charge as soon as the engine is started and run above tickover speed. If the battery is fully charged, it may balance out at zero and may not register at all if the ignition is switched on when the contact breaker points are open and the engine is not running. **SPECIALIST SERVICE.** Any abnormalities in readings will require attention by an electrical specialist. A faulty ammeter cannot be DIY repaired.

29C

☐ Job 30. Clean exhaust system.

TWO-STROKE ENGINES ONLY

Because a two-stroke has a lubrication system in which any excess oil is burnt, the exhaust gas is of a very oily nature. Unless the exhaust system is removed and cleaned out regularly it will eventually clog up, making the engine difficult to start and creating a back pressure that will result in a drop in engine performance. The latter is not easy to detect as it will fall off gradually over an extended period of time.

30A

30A. Two-stroke silencers are made with detachable baffles to aid cleaning them out. Usually the baffles can be removed without having to remove the complete exhaust system or even the silencer. Do so only if the exhaust system is cold otherwise there is risk of burning yourself. If a bolt or screw at the rear of the silencer is removed, the baffle assembly will be released and can be drawn out from the main body.

Cleaning the baffles is a messy job which will necessitate wearing an overall or old clothes, and disposable gloves. Wash the baffles thoroughly with paraffin so that all traces of carbon, oil and sludge are removed. If necessary, finish off by brushing them with a stiff wire brush. If still attached to the machine, it is worth while removing the silencer body too, so that it can be washed out and checked for any holes, splits or rust.

When the parts are clean, allow them to dry off and then reassemble the silencer retaining the baffles with their fixing bolt or screw. **DO NOT UNDER ANY CIRCUMSTANCES RUN THE MACHINE WITHOUT THE BAFFLES IN THE SILENCER OR MODIFY THE BAFFLES IN ANY WAY.** The exhaust system of a two-stroke is designed so that not only does it silence the exhaust effectively but also has an extractor effect to boost performance. A much louder exhaust note does not imply more power - in almost every case the power output will be seriously reduced if the exhaust system set up is tampered with in any way. An unwarranted change of silencer, or a replica of the original will often have a similar effect due to differences in the design of the internal baffles.

It was suggested earlier that the complete exhaust system is removed. While it is unlikely the exhaust pipe has suffered a build up of oil and carbon internally, its removal will provide the opportunity to inspect the exhaust ports of the engine. Carbon will build up in them too and should be cleared away. Engines have been known to run with the ports so full of carbon that there is only a tiny area through which the exhaust gases can escape. The effect on performance under these circumstances will be obvious.

When refitting the exhaust system, make sure all the joints are tight and well sealed. An air leak at any point will cause backfiring in the silencer, which often proves difficult to track down. A vulnerable area is where the exhaust pipe enters the cylinder barrel. If it is retained by either an externally or internally threaded ring, make sure the ring is tightened fully and check it after the first long run. If the ring works loose, it will chatter the thread away and eventually fail to retain the exhaust pipe. To reclaim the thread is an expensive proposition.

If the silencer is of the non-detachable type it can be cleaned out only by flushing it through many times with a paraffin (kerosene).

SAFETY FIRST!
Old instruction books often recommend an alternative method that requires the use of caustic soda, an effective but hazardous chemical to use. As its name suggests, it is both poisonous and highly corrosive, causing severe burns that will prove difficult to heal if it is spilt on the skin. We strongly recommend this method should not be used as apart from personal danger there is the problem of disposing of the spent fluid after it has been drained off, without harming the environment. It is worth noting that a solution of caustic soda should not be used UNDER ANY CIRCUM-STANCES where aluminium is present, as it attacks this metal vigorously, to produce explosive hydrogen gas.

FOUR-STROKE ENGINES ONLY

It is unlikely a four-stroke exhaust system will need cleaning out, even after an extensive period, as the exhaust gases are relatively free from oil compared to those of a two-stroke. It is, however, just as important that the joints of the entire system are kept air-tight as four-stroke engines seem more susceptible to backfiring if air can leak in at any point. Unwarranted changes of silencer may adversely affect performance, some machines being more sensitive to this than others.

30B. It follows also that if a threaded ring or a stub is used where the exhaust pipe enters the cylinder head, it must be kept tight. Threaded rings and stubs are renowned for working loose on some models, with disastrous long term damage that will necessitate an expensive cylinder head repair. Use a high temperature sealant on the threads of a ring before tightening it and if a stub shows signs of working loose, peg it in some way. Alternatively, with twin pipe systems, the rings can be lock-wired together so that one will prevent the other from working loose.

Job 31. Change gearbox oil

Assuming the machine is not a unit-construction model, in which the engine and gearbox share the same oil, the gearbox oil should be changed at the same time.

INSIDE INFORMATION: Although a gearbox holds much less oil than an engine's oil tank or oil compartment, it is more easily contaminated, especially if the clutch operating cable enters it vertically. Unless the cable is adequately shrouded at its lower end, water will enter the gearbox quite easily by running down the cable, to form a corrosive emulsion with the oil.

30B

31A. Remove the gearbox drain plug from the underside, after placing a container below it that will hold more than the gearbox's oil capacity. Allow sufficient time for it to drain completely, then replace and tighten the drain plug after fitting a new fibre sealing washer. Add the correct amount of oil of the recommended viscosity, which will have to be added slowly due to the restricted opening of the filler. With the machine standing vertically, remove the level plug which is usually found towards the rear of the gearbox outer end cover. Allow the excess oil to drain off before replacing the level plug fitted with a new sealing washer.

31B. INSIDE INFORMATION: i) Some gearboxes are difficult to fill, especially the gearbox fitted to the early post-war BSA singles. The circular threaded cap that acts as the combined filler and oil level guide makes refilling or topping up quite difficult, unless a chute of some kind is made down which the oil can be poured very slowly. An alternative and better method is to lean the machine over so that it rests on the left-hand footrest and pour the oil in directly - or do both, as shown here!

31C. INSIDE INFORMATION (contd.): If the threaded cap is then screwed in until the machine is righted and put on to its centre stand, the cap can then be unscrewed to let any excess oil drain off. Don't forget to tighten the cap firmly when the oil level is correct and no more will drain out. ii) Early Burman gearboxes were filled with grease and many owners have found it more convenient to fill them instead with a heavy grade of oil after cleaning out all the grease from their internals. A heavy grade of oil lessens the risk of leakage as these gearboxes were not too well sealed.

☐ Job 32. Change front fork oil.

An even smaller quantity of damping oil is contained in each fork leg of a telescopic front fork. It can therefore become more easily contaminated by water vapour or condensation than the oil in either an oil tank or oil compartment, or in a gearbox.

32A. Place the machine on its centre stand, or front wheel stand, if fitted. It will be very unstable on the latter, which is intended for emergency use only, so in either case give the machine extra support to prevent it from moving forward or toppling over. Raise the front wheel off the ground if it is not already clear, and remove the drain plug from the bottom of each fork leg and slacken the caps in the top of the telescopic fork legs, to prevent air lock. You will need to place a small container under each to catch the oil. When the oil has drained off, lower the machine on to its wheels and depress the front fork several times to make sure all the old oil is expelled.

32A

32B. Raise the machine again on to its stand and unscrew the cap in the top of each fork leg. Some will come away completely, others will remain attached to the damper rod.

32C. Replace the drain plug in each fork leg after fitting a new sealing washer and pour the correct amount of oil of the recommended viscosity into each fork leg, usually a quite small amount. Allow it to drain to the bottom of the fork legs...

32D. ...then replace and tighten the cap in the top of each fork leg.

SPECIALIST SERVICE. A few early post-war models have a telescopic front fork without drain plugs. Under these circumstances the individual fork legs will have to be detached from the steering head assembly and upended to drain off the old oil, unfortunately necessitating a considerable amount of work. This is best entrusted to a dealer or a trained mechanic as special service tools may be required.

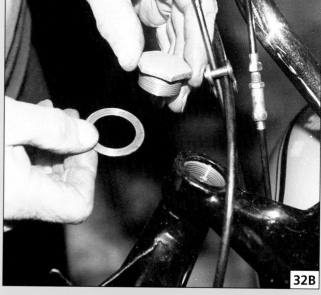

32B

32C

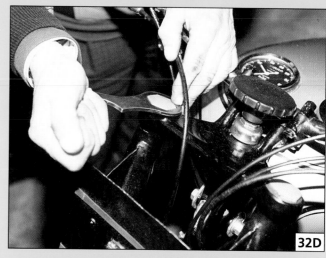

32D

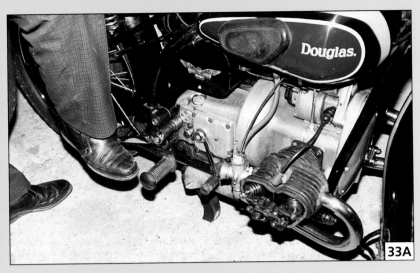

33A

☐ **Job 33. Check valve clearances.**

FOUR-STROKE ENGINES ONLY

Methods for checking and adjusting the valve clearances of any four stroke engine vary considerably, depending on the type of engine as well as its make. In consequence only a general guide can be given, after separating the type of engine into three different categories: overhead camshaft, overhead valve, and side valve.

33B

33A. In every case the clearances have to be set when the engine is cold unless instructed otherwise by the manufacturer. The engine also has to be on its compression stroke with both valves closed before the precise setting instructions are followed. By taking off the valve cover, removing the spark plug/s if you prefer, and turning the engine over with the bike on its stand, you can easily see when when both valves are fully closed, at which point each tappet will be 'loose' on its valve.

OVERHEAD CAMSHAFT ENGINES - TANK REMOVAL

33B. Start by removing the tank, when necessary. Unbolt the through bolts...

33C

33D

33C. ...and lift each one clear of the tank.

33D. Rubber mounting pads tend to 'stick' - remarkably well in some cases!

33E. After disconnecting the pipework, the tank can now be lifted free.

ADJUSTING OHC VALVE CLEARANCES

33F. Remove the cover(s) (if fitted) over the inlet and exhaust valves to gain access to the adjuster on the end of their respective rockers. After checking that both valves are closed, a feeler gauge of the correct thickness is slid between the end of the valve and the adjustable pad that presses on it. After slackening the adjuster lock nut, the correct clearance can be obtained by screwing the pad up or down (in this case, it's with a second spanner) until the feeler gauge is a good sliding fit. The adjuster lock nut should then be tightened and the gap re-checked before attention is given to the other valve. If the cover(s) have to be replaced, fit a new gasket to each.

33G. On this Sunbeam engine, the locknut (B) has a hexagonal head, while the adjuster screw is square - there should be the correct spanner in the tool kit. On a twin, you can be certain that each inlet valve is fully closed when its 'twin' inlet valve is fully open. The same applies to the exhaust valves. Adjust the valves when each one if fully closed.

IMPORTANT NOTE: An exception to these methods of adjustment occurs in the case of the Velocette KSS model. Adjustment is simplified by slackening the lock nuts around each eccentrically-mounted rocker pin then turning the head of each pin to arrive at the correct gap between the end of the valve and the adjustable pad. Turning them inwards decreases the clearance. An arrow is stamped on the rocker pin heads and it is important the arrows should point toward each other after the clearances have been set correctly and the lock nuts re-tightened. If this precaution is not taken, the rockers will not contact the ends of the valves correctly and put a side thrust on the valve guides, causing them to wear rapidly.

ADJUSTMENT OF REAR CYLINDER INLET VALVE CLEARANCE

ADJUST OVERHEAD VALVE ENGINES' VALVE CLEARANCES

33H. Remove the inspection cap, keeping hold of the fibre sealing washer.

33I. Slip the correct thickness of feeler gauge into the gap, once you have ensured that the valve is fully closed (not fully open! - see 33F and 33G). The feeler gauge goes in at a very odd angle on this Triumph!

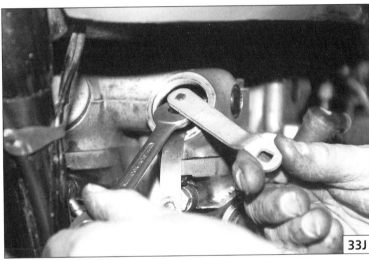

33J. Adjust the gap, as described earlier, until the gauge will just slide nicely in the gap with a touch of resistance, but without being forced.

33K. On this BSA, adjustment is made at the bottom of the pushrod, after removing this access plate.

33L. Three hands are called for once again!

33M. On a horizontally-opposed twin, remove the rocker cover. Often a special tool (an extra wide-blade DIY 'screwdriver' will do nicely) will be needed to remove the retaining screw. (Note: nearly all - but *not all* - bikes have a rocker cover.)

33M

33N. Follow the rules, as before and especially see 33G to work out when each valve is fully closed. Note that turning the engine over will be *much* easier with the spark plugs out!

33O. INSIDE INFORMATION: The B32/B34 Gold Star BSAs have an alternative eccentric rocker pin form of adjustment, behind the oil unions on the left-hand side of the cylinder head.

More care is needed with this type of engine as some are fitted with what are known as ramp cams. With this arrangement, used to quieten an engine by gradually taking up the valve clearance, the correct setting can only be made when one of the valves is in a carefully set position while the other valve clearance is being checked. It is important the manufacturer's recommendations are observed in this respect or there is risk of a valve not seating correctly when the engine is hot and compression being lost. The use of ramp cams is sometimes indicated by a symbol looking like a spoked wheel, stamped on the crankcase after the engine number.

33N

ADJUST SIDE VALVE ENGINES' VALVE CLEARANCES

33P. It is much easier to check the valve clearances of a side valve engine because better access is available to the adjusters. They will be found just above the engine's timing chest, after removing a cover sealed by a gasket. They are, in effect, at the end of the short push rods and bear directly on the ends of the valve stems.

Always make sure the lock nuts on the end of each adjuster are tightened fully after the clearances have been set and re-check the gap with the valves in the same position. Use a new gasket when fitting the valve cover(s).

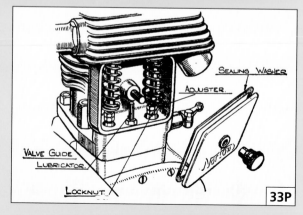

33O

ALL TYPES OF FOUR-STROKE ENGINE

INSIDE INFORMATION: Valve clearances increase as the result of wear. This becomes noticeable through an increase in the engine's mechanical noise. If the clearances decrease, this can be a sign that unleaded petrol (gasoline) is being used in an engine suitable only for leaded fuel. Unleaded fuel causes valve seat recession because the untreated seats are no longer lubricated by lead in the fuel. (Modern engines have special valve seats to prevent damage.) It will result in loss of compression when the valves no longer seat correctly in their closed position.

33P

☐ Job 34. Renew spark plug(s).

A sparking plug has a nominal life of 12,000 miles, but there is advantage in renewing it more frequently to ensure the ignition system operates at its peak condition. The replacement plug must be of the correct grade specified by either the machine's or the sparking plug's manufacturer. If the machine has more than one cylinder, renew all the plugs at the same time and make sure each is re-connected to its correct plug lead.

Before fitting a new sparking plug, first check that its gap corresponds with the recommendations for the type of ignition system fitted to the machine. Coat the threads of the plug with a light smear of graphite grease before re-fitting and tighten it sufficiently to crush its sealing washer and make it seat correctly. Take care NOT to over-tighten, especially if the machine has a light alloy cylinder head.

12,000 Miles or Every Twenty Four Months, Whichever Comes First

First carry out Jobs 2 to 4, 6, 8 to 13, 16, 18 to 34.

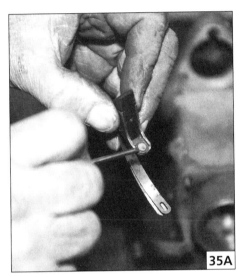

35A

☐ Job 35. Renew contact breaker points.

35A. The contact breaker points need to be in good condition for the ignition system to function at peak efficiency. Even if the points are clean or can be cleaned easily, there may still be need to change them as the result of electrical erosion. This can be identified by looking closely at the surface of the points, using a magnifying glass if necessary. Erosion has occurred if one point has a blister on its surface, which corresponds with a pit in the point face with which it makes contact.

35B. When points show this form of defect, they must be renewed. On ignition systems fitted with a rotating armature magneto of the circular cam ring type, this will mean removing the complete contact breaker assembly by unscrewing the centre bolt or screw...

35C. ...and pulling it from the centre of the armature. There is no fear of the ignition timing being lost, as the contact breaker baseplate has an integral key which locates with a matching slot cut on the inside of the magneto armature shaft. It can be refitted in only the one position.

35B

35C

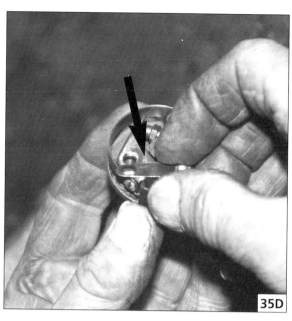

35D. The rocker arm that has the fixed contact is attached via a curved flat spring (arrowed) to a post on the baseplate, where it is held by a small screw.

35E. Remove the screw with great care while maintaining pressure on the spring, otherwise the screw will fly off into orbit, never to be seen again!

35F. The rocker arm can now be pulled off its pivot and the screw that holds the other end of the spring removed. (Illustration, courtesy Lucas)

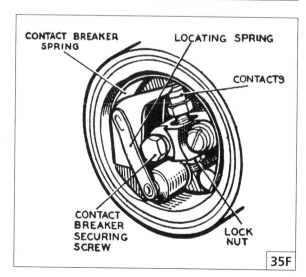

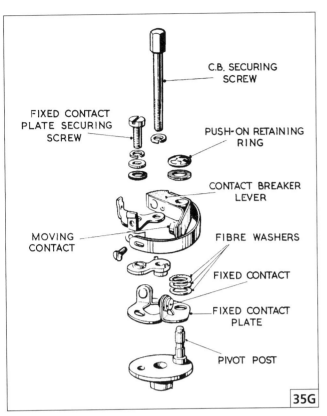

C.B. SECURING SCREW

FIXED CONTACT PLATE SECURING SCREW

PUSH-ON RETAINING RING

CONTACT BREAKER LEVER

MOVING CONTACT

FIBRE WASHERS

FIXED CONTACT

FIXED CONTACT PLATE

PIVOT POST

35G

35G. The adjustable contact breaker point can then be unscrewed, after first slackening its lock nut, or if of a later type, by detaching the fixed plate to which it's attached. And these are the component parts, apparently just about to leave the earth's atmosphere! (Illustration, courtesy Lucas)

35H. The procedure for a magneto fitted with a face cam differs a little. In this case the spring blade to which the fixed point is attached will have to be removed before the centre screw or bolt holding the contact breaker assembly to the armature centre can be unscrewed. It may also be necessary first to bend back the brass tab washer holding the centre screw or bolt tight if one is fitted. When the adjustable point is removed, it will also release the guide around the spring blade. A similar arrangement in the end of the armature to that described above ensures the ignition timing cannot be lost. (Illustration, courtesy Lucas)

35I. ...Remove the screw that has a felt pad on one end...

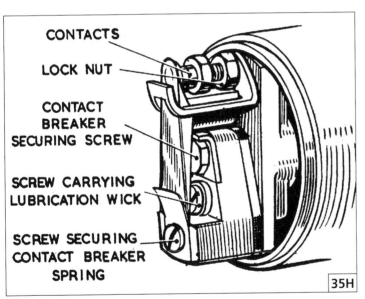

CONTACTS

LOCK NUT

CONTACT BREAKER SECURING SCREW

SCREW CARRYING LUBRICATION WICK

SCREW SECURING CONTACT BREAKER SPRING

35H

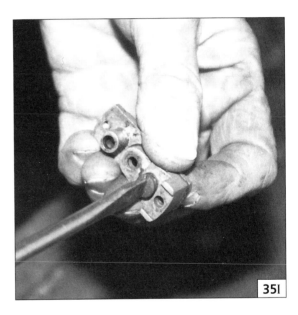

35I

35J

35J. ...and add a couple of drips of light oil before replacing it. Before fitting the new points, make sure their contact surfaces are clean and free from oil or grease. Lightly grease the surface of the cam ring and on the face cam type of assembly, remove the tiny fibre push rod that pushes the points open and grease its whole exterior sparingly before re-inserting it. Also, lightly grease the rocker arm pivot of a magneto of the circular cam ring type.

When re-attaching the rocker arm spring(s) or the spring blade, note that there is an additional short leaf spring. This should be fitted on the underside so that its curved end faces downwards. Pressure must be applied to the spring when re-attaching it to the rocker arm as its tiny retaining screw is fitted and tightened. The hole through which it passes is slotted, so that after assembly the points will line up with each other exactly. This also applies to the spring blade of the face cam type of assembly. The short leaf spring should be fitted at the top, facing upwards.

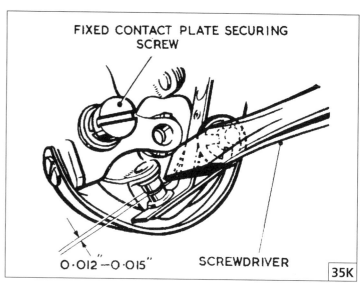

35K. Make sure both screws are tight, re-fit the base-plate to the end of the armature and tighten its retaining bolt or screw, then re-set the contact breaker gap to its recommended setting when the points are in their fully open position. (Illustration, courtesy Lucas)

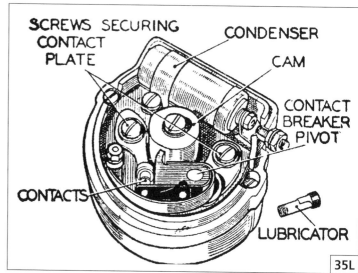

35L. The points fitted to coil ignition systems are very much easier to change and are usually supplied as completely interchangeable assemblies. However, a word of caution is advisable here, as it is very easy to get the arrangement of the separate insulators transposed so that the system will be isolated electrically. This is the Model DK distributor. (Illustration, courtesy Lucas)

35M. Make a careful note of the way in which the insulators are located before you remove the old assembly so that there is no possibility of this happening. You will be sure to forget if you don't! Re-set the gap to the recommended setting when the points are fully open. This is the D1AZ distributor with centrifugal timing advance mechanism. (Illustration, courtesy Lucas)

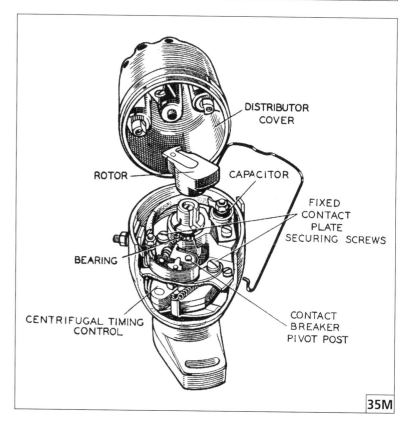

36A

Job 36. Grease wheel bearings.

On later models there was a tendency to pack the wheel bearings with grease when the machine was assembled at the factory. As a result, these wheel hubs are not fitted with a grease nipple so that periodic application of a grease gun cannot be made. Instead, it is necessary to remove the wheel and dismantle the bearing assembly.

SPECIALIST SERVICE. Unless you have experience of dismantling and reassembling wheel bearings, we strongly recommend this job is best left to a dealer or a trained mechanic. If you are competent to tackle this job yourself, however, it is advisable to have a workshop manual or a copy of the manufacturer's original instruction book, which will provide the detailed information. This will identify whether the bearings are retained by a circlip or a threaded locking ring and whether the latter has a left or a right-hand thread.

Wheel bearings can be one of three types, cup and cone, ball roller, or taper roller.

36A. Cup and cone bearings are larger versions of those found on a bicycle and easy to dismantle. After slackening the lock nut that acts also as an adjuster, the cone can be unscrewed from the hub and the spindle withdrawn with the cone on the opposite side still attached. This is best done with the wheel lying flat, as when the cones are removed, the loose ball bearings in each cup will cascade out. The cups can then be driven out of the hub. Remove all the old grease from each bearing assembly and check the cups and the cones for signs of pitting, tracking or other damage. If any such damage is evident, both sets of cups and cones should be renewed and also the ball bearings. Re-pack the bearings with high melting point grease before reassembling; the grease in the cups will help hold the ball bearings in place.

36B. When re-tightening the lock nut on the adjustable cone, there should be a just discernible amount of play at the wheel rim, otherwise a heavy loading will be placed on the bearings, resulting in rapid wear. (Illustration, courtesy Triumph)

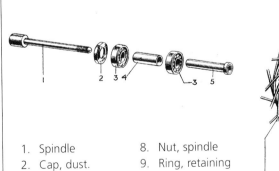

36B

36C. Ball roller bearings are a little more difficult to remove, as the ball races will have to be driven out of the hub after displacing the spacer between them. Wash the bearings in a paraffin (kerosene) bath and check to ensure they have no play in them. They should also be renewed as a pair if the roller tracks are pitted or corroded, or if they make a noise or do not turn freely when they are spun. No play should be discernible at the wheel rim.

1. Spindle
2. Cap, dust.
3. Ball race
4. Tube, distance
5. Sleeve
7. Washer, nut
8. Nut, spindle
9. Ring, retaining
10. Nut, brake drum
11. Lockwasher
12. Hub

36C

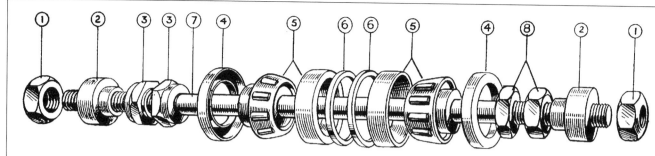

1. Nut spindle
2. Collar, chain adjuster
3. Locknut, anchor plate
4. Cap, dust
5. Bearing, taper roller
6. Ring, backing
7. Spindle
8. Locknut, bearing

36D

36D. Taper roller bearings will come apart much like cup and cone bearings, having one adjustable and one fixed bearing. The outer races will have to be driven out of the hub. The bearings should be examined in a similar way and renewed if any damage is evident. (Illustration, courtesy Triumph)

36E

36E. After reassembly, the lock nut adjuster should be set so that there is a just discernible amount of play at the wheel rim to avoid placing a heavy load on the bearings.

If the hub is still packed with grease there is no need to disturb it. A hub should never be more than 2/3rds full of grease, which should be of the high melting point type.

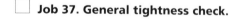

Job 37. General tightness check.

37A. Nuts and bolts tend to work loose due to road shocks and vibration, no matter how well they were tightened originally. Work methodically all around the machine. Pay particular attention to the engine and gearbox mounting bolts and to the head steady, if one is fitted to the cylinder head. If a nut or bolt habitually works loose, there must be a reason. If necessary, ensure it does not happen again by placing a washer or a spring washer beneath the nut and the part with which it makes contact. Alternatively, use one of the proprietary brands of thread lock.

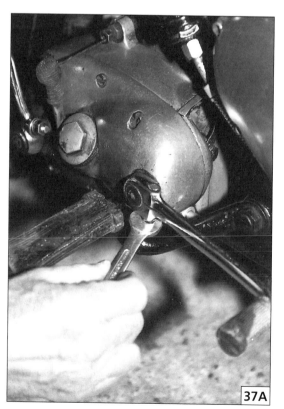

37A

37B. Re-torque the cylinder head - essential about 1,000 miles after an overhaul. On overhead-valve engines, valve clearances will have to be re-adjusted.

INSIDE INFORMATION: Manufacturers have only recently given torque wrench settings. Before that, it was a case of trial and error!

☐ Job 38. Clean battery terminals.

In the early 1950s, electrical systems changed to a positive earth (ground) as it was believed this would overcome the tendency for battery terminals to corrode. Unfortunately, this did not prove very effective and most electrical systems soon changed back to a negative earth to conform with earlier practice.

38A. If the battery terminals repeatedly corrode, remove their connections and clean away every trace of corrosion from the battery terminals and also their connections. The easiest way to do so is to remove the battery, take it out of doors and pour a kettle of very hot water over the corroded terminals. Clean and dry the parts affected and sand off hardened corrosion if necessary, then re-make the connections and coat the terminals and their connections with one of the proprietary products made specifically to prevent corrosion from re-occurring.

38B. Make sure the corrosion did not occur as the result of acid spillage from a cracked seal above the battery's plates, a trapped vent pipe, or loose caps that seal off each battery cell. An excessively high charge from a DC dynamo or an alternator, or due to a faulty voltage regulator unit (shown here), can also cause corrosion by causing the battery acid to 'boil over' and escape through the vents above each cell. This can also apply to a battery that has reached the end of its working life and will no longer hold a charge.

INSIDE INFORMATION: The average life of a motorcycle battery is not more than three years - or much less if it is allowed to vibrate unhindered!

SPECIALIST SERVICE. Re-setting a voltage regulator is a job for a genuine electrical specialist - not a 'bodger' who may make matters worse!

Job 39. Check steering damper.

39A. Many of the older machines will have a steering damper of the friction type fitted, especially if the machine has been used for hauling a sidecar. Make sure the handlebars still turn freely from lock to lock with the steering damper fully slackened off. Check also that when it is tightened, the handlebars become more difficult to turn.

39B. If the steering damper fails to offer much resistance to turning when it has been tightened, this may have been caused by over-greasing the steering head bearings. Excess grease will run on to the steering damper plates (arrowed) and cause them to slip rather than grip. The long term remedy is to renew the friction plates, but as they may well be unobtainable now, boiling them in water containing a liberal amount of household detergent may suffice after first wiping them clean.

Job 40. Disc brake calliper(s).

DISC BRAKES ONLY

SPECIALIST SERVICE. Disc brake calipers lead a hard life, being fully exposed to the weather and also to debris of various kinds thrown up from the road by the tyres. Apart from any cleaning suggested earlier, now is the time to check that the caliper(s) are still working effectively. If the piston(s) do not relax their grip on the brake pads after the brake is no longer being applied and cleaning their exposed exterior(s) as described in Job 27Y does not help, expert attention is necessary. We strongly recommend that the removal, dismantling and reassembly of a disc brake caliper should be carried out by a trained mechanic or a specialist in this kind of work. Apart from the fact that the hydraulic brake fluid will have to be drained off, later to be replaced and have any air bled out of the system, the whole operation needs to be carried out in scrupulously conditions. The possibility of brake failure due to faulty reassembly or air being trapped in the brake fluid cannot be over-emphasised.

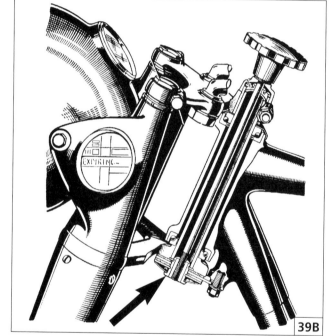

18,000 Miles or Every Three Years, Whichever Comes First

First carry out Jobs 2 to 4, 6, 8 to 13, 16, 18 to 33, and 37.

Job 41. Electrical wiring and switchgear.

41A.

41B.

41A. The wiring used for a motorcycle's electrical system was at one time of the rubber insulated type. Largely as the result of weathering, the rubber will eventually harden and crack, which will cause the inner wire to be exposed and give rise to short circuits or even a fire - especially dangerous where it touches metalwork, as here. The outer rubber coating will also swell and disintegrate if it comes into contact with petrol (gasoline) or oil, and fail in a similar manner.

41B. In more recent years, wire with a plastic (PVC) outer covering has been used, which deteriorates much less rapidly but can still age-harden as time progresses and can still pull out of connections, leaving bare ends.

41C.

SAFETY FIRST!
If the wiring is starting to show signs of deterioration, the entire wiring loom should be renewed, a not inconsiderable task. It is possible to obtain a complete replacement loom for many of the machines no longer in production. Don't be tempted to carry out a 'patch' repair yourself by cutting out the damaged section and replacing it with a new piece of wire. By making additional joints it is easy to create a high resistance unless each joint is expertly made. In addition, poor lighting on many machines can more often than not be attributed to amateur modifications of this nature or to poor connections at terminals.

41C. Check each wire visually along its entire length, even if this necessitates removing the petrol tank to do so. Trouble in this area is the more unlikely, as the wires will be enclosed within an outer sheath that gives them additional protection. The vulnerable places are where the wires emerge from the sheath (especially in the vicinity of the steering head) or where they tend to rub against any metal part or pass through a hole that is not fitted with an insulating rubber grommet. Any wire that is subjected to constant flexing is particularly prone to fracture, a fault that is very difficult to detect if the outer rubber or plastic covering has remained intact.

INSIDE INFORMATION: If you decide to re-wire the machine yourself, make sure you get the loom that corresponds with the make and model. Start by disconnecting the battery and do not re-connect it until the entire system has been re-wired and you are sure every connection has been correctly made. Wiring looms usually have colour-coded sleeves at the end of each wire, or wires of different colours with an identifiable tracer colour as an aid to making the correct connections. The connection colours should correspond with those of the wiring diagram in the owner's handbook or a workshop manual.

41D. INSIDE INFORMATION: Some on/off road competition models, such as the Triumph Trophy Twins, have a plug and socket connection in the underside of the headlamp, so that the latter can be removed with ease. The plug is prone to working loose so that without warning the entire lighting system is plunged into darkness. It is wise to tape the plug very firmly to its socket so that there is no possibility of this happening.

41E. Little can be done to repair a broken headlamp switch apart from cleaning the contacts. Proprietary aerosol-type contact cleaners are available for this purpose, which can be used without need to dismantle the switch. Otherwise the switch will have to be renewed, assuming a replacement of the correct type can be found. Many different types of switch were used during the period this book covers. This one is shown in a proprietary Lucas panel removed from the headlamp. (Illustration, courtesy Lucas)

INSIDE INFORMATION: Some headlamp switches also incorporate an ignition switch in their centre. If the key is missing or has been lost, this is no real problem as the keys were not cut individually like those of a car. It is even possible to operate the switch with a knife blade or even a screwdriver in an emergency!

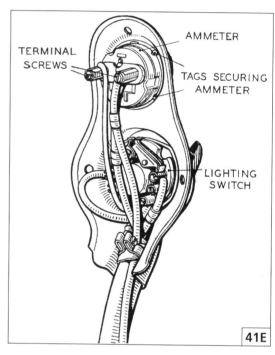

41F. A dipswitch will often fail because the spring-loaded moving arm inside seizes up. It can usually be freed by the application of an aerosol-type contact cleaner or a WD40 spray after removing it from the handlebars.

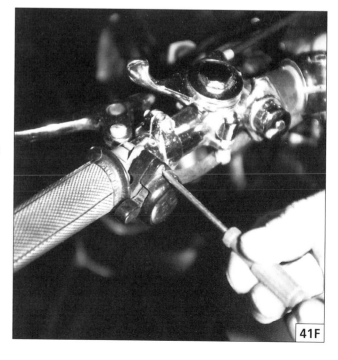

Job 42. Check crankcase breather pipes.

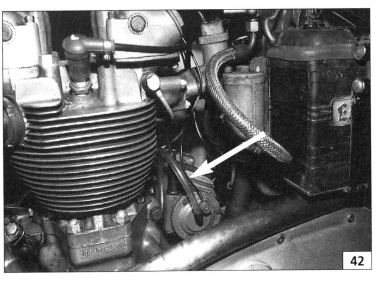

42. Most machines have a crankcase breather of some kind, which is operated mechanically by the engine. It usually vents to the atmosphere via a plastic pipe (arrowed). Check that the pipe is not blocked, otherwise the now sealed system will encourage oil leaks from various parts of the engine. This also applies to the contact breaker cover of a magneto, which has a very small hole bored in it. If it is blocked, the points surfaces will get tarnished, resulting in a misfire or even a complete ignition failure.

Job 43. Compression test.

It was not usual for manufacturers to quote the minimum acceptable figure for the compression pressure in each cylinder, as it is today. In consequence it will be necessary for the rider to decide whether or not the cylinder appears to have ample compression. As a rough guide, on most large capacity singles it should be possible to put full weight on the kickstarter for a short period before it starts to go down, assuming the engine is on the compression stroke with both valves closed.

Compression is more difficult to judge on multi-cylinder machines, those of small capacity, and two-strokes. If the kickstarter offers virtually no resistance at all, the probability is that the engine is in need of an overhaul. Additional signs are the discharge of oil in significant quantity from the crankcase breather, the heavy consumption of oil, and a tendency for the exhaust to produce more white or blue-coloured smoke than usual - the last not so easy to identify on a two-stroke.

Job 44. Renew hydraulic brake fluid.

DISC BRAKES ONLY

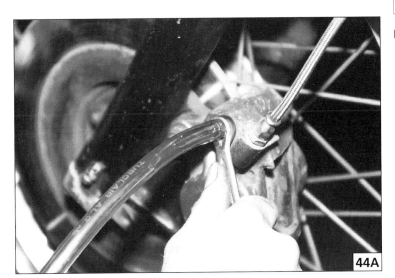

SAFETY FIRST! AND SPECIALIST SERVICE Obviously, your bikes brakes are among its most important safety related items. Do NOT dismantle or attempt to perform any work on the braking system unless you are fully competent to do so. If you have not been trained in this work, but wish to carry it out, it is ESSENTIAL that you have a garage or qualified mechanic check your work before using the vehicle on the road. See also the section on BRAKES AND ASBESTOS in Chapter 1, Safety First! for further information.

It is necessary to change the hydraulic brake fluid at regular intervals as it is hygroscopic - it absorbs water vapour from the atmosphere. As a result, under heavy braking, brakes can fail totally and without warning. Never use anything but the recommended specification of hydraulic brake fluid, from a fresh sealed container. You should never use fluid drained off after the brakes have been bled, as it will contain minute trapped bubbles of air and moisture.

44A. To drain the system, remove the cap from the brake fluid reservoir, take off the dust cap from the drain (bleed) valve on the caliper, and clean around it.

44B. Attach a short length of clear plastic tubing to the valve and arrange it so that one end is immersed in new hydraulic brake fluid contained in a glass jar. The plastic tube must remain below the level of the fluid throughout the entire operation, otherwise air will enter the system to create further problems.

Open the nipple by unscrewing it about one turn, with the plastic

18,000 MILE SERVICE

pipe still attached. Operate the brake lever and continue to do so until all the fluid has drained from the system. Close the nipple, still leaving the plastic tube attached and drain off the excess fluid in the glass jar. Leave sufficient to keep the end of the plastic tube submerged when the jar is placed back in position again.

Fill the reservoir with new hydraulic brake fluid, open the nipple again and pump the brake lever until the fluid flowing from the nipple, through the plastic tube, is seen to contain no air bubbles. Maintain a close check on the reservoir all the time and top it up if necessary. Air can enter here too if the reservoir is allowed to run dry. When fluid only is expelled, close the nipple, take off the plastic tube, and remove the glass jar. If the job has been carried out correctly, application of the brake lever should apply the brake firmly, with no sign of sponginess. If there is, repeat the bleeding operation to permit any residual air to be displaced.

SAFETY FIRST!
i) If brake fluid should come into contact with the skin or eyes, rinse immediately with plenty of water. ii) It is acceptable for the brake fluid level to fall slightly during normal use, but if it falls significantly below the bottom of the filler cap neck, it indicates a leak or an internal seal failure. Stop using the bike and seek specialist advice immediately. iii) If you get dirt into the hydraulic system it can cause brake failure. Wipe the filler cap clean before removing. iv) You should only ever use only new brake fluid from an air-tight container. Old fluid absorbs moisture and this could cause the brakes to fail when carrying out an emergency stop or other heavy use of the brakes - just when you need them most and are least able to do anything about it, in fact!

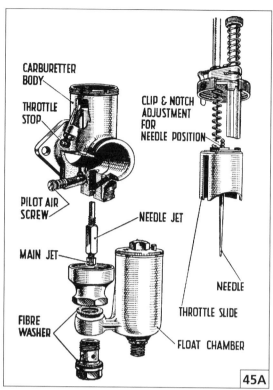

45A

☐ **Job 45. Clean and check carburettor(s).**

45A. Remove the carburettor(s) from the machine after first detaching the petrol (gasoline) pipes and unscrewing the threaded ring at the top(s) so that the throttle slide(s) and throttle valve assembly(ies) can be withdrawn. Illustrated is the Amal Type 6 carburettor with its separate float chamber.

45B. Most four-stroke models were fitted with a carburettor(s) of Amal manufacture, and Villiers-engined two-strokes with a carburettor of that company's own manufacture.

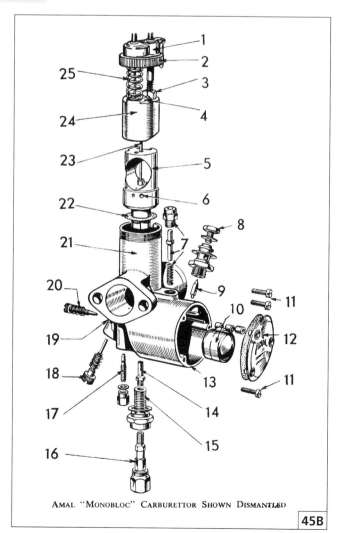

AMAL "MONOBLOC" CARBURETTOR SHOWN DISMANTLED

45B

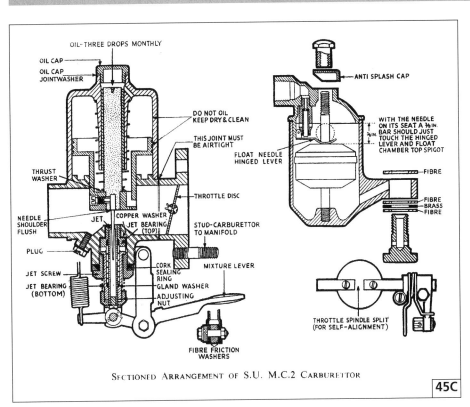

OIL-THREE DROPS MONTHLY
OIL CAP
OIL CAP JOINTWASHER
DO NOT OIL KEEP DRY & CLEAN
THIS JOINT MUST BE AIRTIGHT
THRUST WASHER
FLOAT NEEDLE HINGED LEVER
NEEDLE SHOULDER FLUSH
JET   COPPER WASHER
JET BEARING (TOP)
THROTTLE DISC
STUD-CARBURETTOR TO MANIFOLD
PLUG
CORK SEALING RING
MIXTURE LEVER
JET SCREW
GLAND WASHER
JET BEARING (BOTTOM)
ADJUSTING NUT
FIBRE FRICTION WASHERS

ANTI SPLASH CAP
WITH THE NEEDLE ON ITS SEAT A 3⁄8 IN. BAR SHOULD JUST TOUCH THE HINGED LEVER AND FLOAT CHAMBER TOP SPIGOT
FIBRE
FIBRE BRASS FIBRE

THROTTLE SPINDLE SPLIT (FOR SELF-ALIGNMENT)

Sectioned Arrangement of S.U. M.C.2 Carburettor

45C

45C. There are, however, a few exceptions. The Ariel Square Four models, for example, had a Solex carburettor, some Triumph T20 Tiger Cub models were fitted with one of Zenith manufacture, and some early Triumph 6T Thunderbird models with an S.U. carburettor (illustrated) made for motorcycle use.

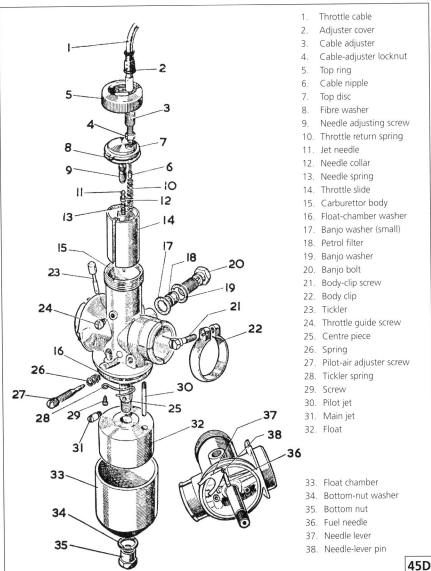

1. Throttle cable
2. Adjuster cover
3. Cable adjuster
4. Cable-adjuster locknut
5. Top ring
6. Cable nipple
7. Top disc
8. Fibre washer
9. Needle adjusting screw
10. Throttle return spring
11. Jet needle
12. Needle collar
13. Needle spring
14. Throttle slide
15. Carburettor body
16. Float-chamber washer
17. Banjo washer (small)
18. Petrol filter
19. Banjo washer
20. Banjo bolt
21. Body-clip screw
22. Body clip
23. Tickler
24. Throttle guide screw
25. Centre piece
26. Spring
27. Pilot-air adjuster screw
28. Tickler spring
29. Screw
30. Pilot jet
31. Main jet
32. Float

33. Float chamber
34. Bottom-nut washer
35. Bottom nut
36. Fuel needle
37. Needle lever
38. Needle-lever pin

45D

45D. It is the float chamber that will first require attention and also any filters at the petrol inlet point, as this is where any dirt or water will tend to collect. It is unlikely any of the jets will be blocked or partially blocked, otherwise the engine would not have run properly. If it is necessary to clear a blocked jet, always do so with a jet of air, such as that from a tyre pump. Never use wire, as this could easily enlarge the size of the hole in the jet and create further problems. Illustrated is the Villiers Type S.19 and S.25 carburettor.

45E. Make sure the slide moves freely inside the carburettor body and is closed by its return spring. Where a separate air slide is fitted, this too must move freely and be fully raised when the air control is open. If it sticks in a partly open position, petrol consumption will rise steeply. If it doesn't fully close, starting from cold may become very difficult.

Check that the jet, needle, and slide sizes are as recommended by the manufacturer. Often, carburettor settings are inadvertently changed to compensate for what may well be an ignition or an engine defect. Check also that the needle is not bent and that the float needle seats correctly so that it cuts off the flow of petrol when the correct level is reached in the float chamber. Obscure problems are sometimes caused by a punctured carburettor float, which admits petrol to change the level at which it will float. This is the Amal Concentric (Mk 1) carburettor.

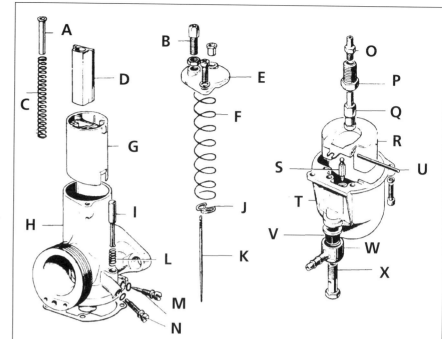

A. Air valve guide sleeve
B. Adjuster
C. Spring
D. Air valve
E. Top
F. Throttle spring
G. Throttle slide
H. Mixture chamber
I. Tickler
J. Needle clip
K. Jet needle
L. Tickler spring

M. Air screw
N. Throttle stop
O. Needle jet
P. Main jet holder
Q. Main jet
R. Float
S. Float needle
T. Bowl
U. Float spindle
V. Filter
W. Banjo
X. Banjo bolt

45E

45F. The parts most likely to wear are the carburettor slide and mixing chamber body, causing the former to rattle about inside the carburettor body and produce an audible 'click' at engine tick-over speeds. Replacement parts for the Amal Monobloc and Concentric carburettors are still readily available from most carburettor specialists, but not so easy to acquire for the earlier types with a separate float chamber.

*INSIDE INFORMATION AND **SPECIALIST SERVICE**: The quality of pattern spares for the latter is variable, so a better alternative is to have the carburettor body bored out and its associated components sleeved to match, restoring them once again to being a good fit. There are several who specialise in reclamation work of this nature. A modern carburettor will also offer a better alternative, but if one of these is fitted it will be instantly recognisable and the machine will lose its originality.*

When reassembling the carburettor(s) make sure the threaded top ring is tightened fully after the slide assembly has been reinserted. If it works lose, the carburettor can jam in the fully open position, with catastrophic results!

45F

INSIDE INFORMATION: Always open the throttle fully and make sure it closes without jamming wide open, before running the engine.

45G. Check that the flange has not become bowed through previous over-tightening of the retaining nuts. If it has, this will be the site of a potential air leak. If necessary, the flange can be filed flat, taking care no metal filings enter the carburettor body, provided you are skilled enough. Otherwise, it's a machine shop, **SPECIALIST SERVICE** job. Always tighten the retaining nuts sufficiently to hold the carburettor firmly. Each should have a spring washer beneath it.

45H. If there is a flanged joint with the manifold, do not overlook the need for the fibre heat-insulating spacer, which should have a new gasket on either side of it.

☐ Job 46. Check petrol tap.

Petrol taps can be divided into two main types, those of the push-pull type with cork inserts, and those of the lever type which rely on a metal to metal seal. The former type may, or may not, have provision for turning on a small amount of reserve fuel when the main supply runs out.

46A. If a tap blocks or has a diminished flow it will be necessary to drain and remove the petrol (gasoline) tank before the tap can be unscrewed from its bottom. Keep well away from any naked flame or other source of heat during removal as inevitably some petrol will still spill out as the tap is removed. Carry out this work out of doors and wear impervious gloves when draining fuel.

46B. The push-pull type is easy to dismantle. A small grub screw in its side will release the push-pull plunger after it is unscrewed. This will expose the cork seal, which is retained by a headed brass rod which will unscrew from the plunger body. If there is a similar plunger at the other end of the tap, one of the two will be acting as the reserve tap.

46B

46C. If the tap has been leaking, the cork seal will have to be renewed. Although these are now difficult to obtain, they are sometimes found at autojumbles or may be listed by some spare parts suppliers. If the machine has been stored for a while, however, the leakage may be due to the fact that the cork has shrunk.

INSIDE INFORMATION: Boiling the corks in water will often bring them back to their correct size and make them usable again.

Lever-type taps are more often found on competition or high performance models, as they are less likely to be turned off accidentally. Their main problem is that if they have not been used for a while they become stiff and very difficult to turn.

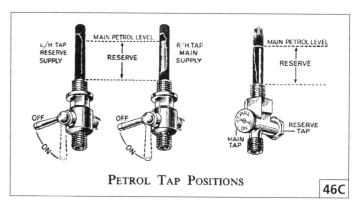

PETROL TAP POSITIONS

46C

46D. All that can be done under these circumstances is to dismantle them and give the taper seal a light coating of grease before reassembly. It is possible to grind in the seating with fine valve grinding paste in an extreme case, but great care needs to be taken not to enlarge the seat or worse still, for traces of abrasive to get into the carburettor.

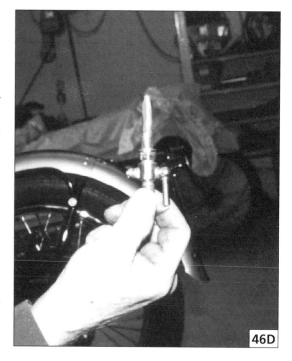

46D

INSIDE INFORMATION: Before screwing the tap back into the petrol tank, check that its protective gauze is clean and that it is not broken at any point. It plays an important role in screening out any larger pieces of rust or debris in the petrol or from the inside of the petrol tank that would otherwise find its way into the carburettor(s). Fit a new sealing washer and be prepared to fit more than one to ensure the tap is in its correct operating position when it is fully tightened.

CHAPTER FOUR
BUYING A CLASSIC BIKE

Part I: The Generation Game

To offer advice about finding and buying a classic bike is fraught with difficulty. Quite apart from the fact that the description itself applies to virtually any motorcycle that has a collector's value, the ultimate decision has to be a personal one, which only the potential buyer can make. Yet this is also the time when advice from others who know the subject well is welcome and frequently sought. Not only can it help in the decision making but it can also highlight some of the pitfalls which may trap the unwary.

The first stage is to decide what age and type of machine is likely to appeal most. Broadly speaking, classic bikes fall conveniently into one of five different categories - veteran, vintage, pre-war, post-war and moderns.

The Veteran Era

Veteran motorcycle covers any machine made up to and including 31st December 1914, including what many regard as the early primitives. It is a classification agreed by the Sunbeam and Vintage Motor Cycle Clubs. Needless to say, the really old machines rarely appear on the market, and when they do, they command a high price. Furthermore, they are not a very practical proposition for riding on today's roads carrying high density traffic. With brakes akin to those found on a bicycle, a low level of performance, and often no clutch or gears, a certain amount of skill is needed to ride them safely within their limitations. Wet weather will induce further problems with belt slip, if the machine has this form of drive, and when steep hills are encountered the rider will soon find out why pedals were fitted! Indeed, on some machines the rider may even have to dismount and run alongside it to keep the engine running!

1. Spare parts in usable condition will prove almost impossible to obtain, even for the more common models of this era such as Triumph and Douglas, to say nothing of some of the more obscure models. This for instance, is an example of an early veteran: a true 'primitive', with its bicycle-type frame and

rudimentary drive. (Although the engine is inscribed 'The Brutus', it is basically a Quadrant). Most replacement parts will have to be specially made, which can prove expensive as they will be one-off items. By far the greatest problem, however, arises in knowing whether or not a machine still closely adheres to the manufacturer's original specification. There has always been a tendency for owners to modify their motorcycles as they get older, so that they keep up with the times. It was also possible for the purchaser of a new machine to request certain changes in specification by paying extra, or for a manufacturer to fit alternative components from a different parts supplier if the parts normally fitted as standard were temporarily out of stock. All this makes it increasingly more difficult to know whether a machine offered for sale is genuine or not. Fortunately there is a convenient way of finding this out.

2. Any machine manufactured before 31st December 1914 can be registered with the Sunbeam Motor Cycle Club. A specially appointed committee will scrutinise the completed application form and the two obligatory

photographs, one of each side of the machine, supplied by the applicant. If it conforms to their exacting requirements, they will issue a Pioneer Machine Certificate and enter the machine's details in the club's Pioneer Machine Register. Not only does the certificate authenticate the date of the machine and confirm its specification is correct but it will also be eligible to take part in the club's annual Pioneer Run from Epsom Downs to Brighton. So, if a machine is offered for sale with a Sunbeam MCC Pioneer Machine Certificate, it can be assumed it is a genuine veteran.

Vintage Machines and the 1930s

A vintage motorcycle is defined as one made during the period 1st January 1915 to 31st December 1930, a period also accepted by the Sunbeam and Vintage MCCs.

Strangely enough, in spite of the First World War, the manufacture of motorcycles for civilian use was continued until 15th February 1917. Many of these machines were virtually identical to those that were being made when Britain declared war on Germany in 1914, so this is a somewhat grey area where some have been passed off as genuine veterans. They are very hard to detect, so special care needs to be exercised, especially if the machine has nothing to authenticate its date of manufacture.

When production for the civilian market resumed after the war, the early post-war models were very similar to their pre-war predecessors, although most incorporated some modifications to update them. They can still prove something of a liability in today's traffic, even though the widespread use of a countershaft gearbox made pedals a superfluous requirement. It was not until the mid to late twenties that significant advances in design became evident. All chain transmission, overhead valve engines and internal expanding hub brakes all combined to make these later models much easier, safer, and more pleasant to ride. Frame and fork improvements were made at the same time, to cope with the higher performance from overhead valve and overhead camshaft engines. From about 1927 onwards, the vintage motorcycle was beginning to look much like the motorcycle we take for granted today. Wired-on tyres were replacing the old beaded edge type and electric lighting was superseding the old acetylene lights. Towards the end of this era, chromium plating was beginning to replace the nickel plating that had been used for so long. It was more durable, provided a much more attractive finish, and was easier to keep clean.

3. As an example of vintage machinery, few would doubt that this 1929 M10 500cc overhead camshaft AJS is a most attractive and desirable model. And indeed, many regard this as the 'Golden Era' of motorcycling and find vintage models have a particular attraction due to their excellent performance resulting from a favourable power to weight ratio. Sadly, they are getting scarce now, especially the so-called flat tank models with their distinctive appearance. The higher performance models tend to attract the higher prices, although

their once very popular side valve counterparts offer attractive motorcycling with more economic running costs. Much the same problem persists here too, as it is often very difficult to tell a 1930 from a 1931 model. The equivalent certification scheme is a listing in the Vintage Motor Cycles Club's Machine Register after a machine's details and photographs have been verified by a Marque Specialist. Bona fide 1930 models are eligible to take part in some events open to veteran and vintage machines only, such as the Vintage MCC's annual Banbury Run.

The Pre-War Era

4. Although this book is primarily about classic British 'bikes, there is a small number of foreign pre-war 'bikes around. Not many of the pre-war Indian models were imported into the UK from the USA during the 30s, especially the rare 1265cc four cylinder model.

Pre-war models are regarded under the guidelines of the Vintage MCC as having been made during the period 1st January 1931 to 31st December 1945. It included the models made for use by the armed forces and other wartime organisations. Many of the machines of this era were manufactured during the depression of the early 1930s, when they were hard to sell. Quite a few were built to a price, to undercut that of a rival model made by a competitor, to help keep its manufacturer in business. Because of this, some consider pre-war machines are barely worth much attention, as they regard them as of inferior quality. However, this would seem to be a somewhat flawed outlook as it could be argued very convincingly that a number of outstanding models were launched during this period. It could certainly not be said that the Ariel Square Four or the first of the Triumph Twins failed to make any impact!

Post-Second World War

5. The next category comprises the post-war models, and runs from 1st January 1946 to 31st December 1960, again following Vintage MCC guidelines. It is this class of machine and the one that follows that has attracted most attention during recent years.

Lucky is the person who found this 1946 348cc 'garden gate' Manx Norton. It had a racing history too, having been ridden in the 1946 Manx Grand Prix by Tommy McEwan. From the beginning of this period more attention was given to rider and passenger comfort, which commenced with the widespread acceptance of the telescopic front fork by 1948. It was followed soon after by some form of rear suspension, when manufacturers realised this was regarded as equally desirable by riders and made a strong selling point. It was during this period that Continental machines began to be imported in large numbers, mostly of German or Italian origin, so they become part of the scene too. When this period was almost at its very end, the first Japanese models made their impact. They broke with conventional design and offered something that was quite different yet had its own appeal.

This recent peak of interest can be attributed in many cases to 'born again' motorcyclists returning to their former love. Many who had been ardent riders had to revert to four wheels by force of circumstances when they married and raised a family. When the children grew up and there was more disposable income available, they bought a motorcycle, which they used solely for leisure purposes. Often, it was a similar or later version of a machine they had owned in the past, such was the lure of nostalgia.

The 'Classic' Era

Later machines are also given the title 'classic', a term which lends itself to interpretation in so many different ways. The guidelines devised by the Vintage MCC are somewhat flexible as although they regard this period as beginning on 1st January 1961, there is a 'rolling' closing date. This is because under the club's rules any machine more than 25 years old qualifies at present. Needless to say there has been a great deal of controversy over the acceptance of these later machines, a high proportion of which are of Japanese origin. The controversy still continues as many competitive events are becoming overwhelmed with the later models. Not unexpectedly, these more sophisticated models put their earlier

counterparts at a disadvantage by competing with them on level terms. How and when the current situation will be resolved is anyone's guess. At the very least it would seem pertinent to adopt a handicap system so that the older machines stand a better chance.

It must be emphasised that the classes of machine outlined above are those recognised in the UK by the Sunbeam and Vintage MCCs. Many other clubs, especially those based overseas, may decide differently, though mostly with regard to the deadlines for the more modern classes. At least one club operates on the basis that if you regard your machine as a classic, you can ride it in our events regardless of its age! The organisers of classic bike shows may also have their own ideas on the above demarcation lines.

6. Though not yet admissible as a 'classic' under the Vintage MCC's present dating policy, it may well be regarded as one in the future. It is the 1987 reincarnation of the Matchless G80, using an ohc Rotax four valve single cylinder engine.

Part II: Finding The Right Bike

Having more or less made up your mind about what sort of classic bike you would like to purchase, the next question is how to find one. Reading the advertisements in the local newspaper or in any of the classic motorcycling magazines is the most obvious move as they will give you an idea not only of what is available but also the prices being asked. In this latter respect, a Buyers Guide with a recommended price band that will prove very helpful can be found in *Classic Bike Guide*.

Advertisements

Don't take for granted the prices asked in the private advertisement columns, as the advertiser may be 'flying a kite' to try and obtain a figure above that normally expected. Beware of buying a machine imported into the UK unless there is evidence to prove all import duties have been paid.

Treat with suspicion advertisements that mention a machine has been fully reconditioned or was once owned by a well-known personality, unless there is written confirmation of this. Receipts should be available for a machine that has been extensively restored, relating to all the new parts purchased and any work carried out by a specialist. Remember also that engineering standards

vary enormously. What one owner may regard as good may well be considered deplorable by the machine's next owner. Any machine with a 'history' should have adequate documentation to support this, preferably not in photocopy form. It follows, of course, that there should be some evidence to confirm the vendor is the actual owner of the machine being sold, in view of the large number of thefts now taking place.

There are a number of specialist dealers in classic bikes who regularly advertise in the classic bike magazines. Their prices are likely to be higher than those asked by the individual advertiser, as they have much higher overheads. However, it should be borne in mind that they will be more discerning in what they buy-in to safeguard their reputation, unless they are selling on the behalf of a third party on a 'sale or return' basis. They should be prepared to 'see you right' if what you buy from them is not up to the standard you would reasonably expect. Recommendations from those who have bought from the dealer before will prove useful in this respect. Don't buy over the 'phone, however, without first having seen the machine. You could have a nasty surprise when the machine arrives!

Auctions and Clubs

7. You don't often see a Brough Superior at an auction, but this 1936 SS80 sold for £2,050 at a September 1983 Palmer Snell auction at Shepton Mallet. Auctions offer

yet another alternative method of purchasing a classic bike, although you should be aware whether or not you have to pay a buyer's premium on the hammer price, which can often inflate it significantly. Remember the data supplied in the auction catalogue is closely based on that supplied by the vendor. Although the more reputable auctioneers will have an independent expert verify its accuracy, they cannot be held responsible for any unintentional errors or lapses. Make a very detailed inspection of the machine before you decide to bid for it and do not go ahead if there is anything that dissatisfies you. Don't be afraid to ask for a second opinion (assuming whoever you ask is not also likely to bid for it!) and as far as possible, take a knowledgeable friend with you. The same cautions about authentication mentioned in the paragraph above apply equally well here.

8. Possibly the best action you can take is first to join the one-make club relating to the marque of machine in which you are interested, or the Vintage Motor Cycle Club if you are seeking an older one. Clubs such as these have their own magazines with an advertisement section listing members machines available

for sale. Prices are likely to be much fairer and the advertiser is likely to know much more about the machine and to have looked after it better. You will also learn from the magazine about the foibles of the individual models, which every machine has!

So far it has been assumed the purchase of a complete machine in running order has been the intention. However, what about the type of machine in 'as found' condition that requires complete restoration, or one that has been completely dismantled, its parts scattered amongst a number of boxes?

Restoration Projects

A machine requiring complete restoration often offers a very satisfactory way of acquiring a classic bike cheaply - on the assumption that it can be purchased at a realistic figure. Unfortunately, many vendors are led to believe that any old machine is worth a small fortune, irrespective of whether or not it has to be totally restored. They have no comprehension of what it costs to restore an old motorcycle, even if the purchaser has the facilities and experience to undertake most of the work. Farming it out for a specialist to restore will prove an expensive proposition. One professional restorer said recently words to the effect that you should decide how much you can afford to spend, double the sum, and multiply the time it will take by a factor of four and you will not

be far out! This is not an intended 'dig' at restorers - far from it. Many turn out a really first-class job and show real dedication. But like everything else, if you ask for expert attention, you must expect to pay the expert's price.

One advantage in purchasing a derelict or unrestored but complete classic bike is that it will be all in one piece so that you can make notes and take photographs to ensure it is reassembled correctly after restoration. In addition, any parts that are beyond redemption, such as pressed steel chaincases, mudguards etc, will be available for use as a pattern to help locate replacements or to have replicas made.

Motorcycles that have been completely dismantled can be a real headache as you will be purchasing what is, in effect, the pieces of a huge jigsaw. You will have no guide to what the machine looked like originally if the vendor has no photographs of it, having to rely instead on contemporary illustrations. One might well ask why it was taken apart - often because it was completely worn out or because some vital but irreplaceable part has broken and cannot be repaired or replaced. Furthermore, you will have no idea how many parts are missing, or even if parts from another machine have been mixed in. It is our recommendation that you think long and hard about taking on a do-it-yourself project of this nature, even if its price is attractive. You could be heading for endless trouble.

Machines found in a derelict or completely dismantled condition usually have never been recorded on the DVLC computer or its equivalent in another country, so a V5 or similar registration document will not be available. Fortunately, this is no longer the deterrent it once was as in the UK the DVLC's rules relating to the re-registration of machines like these have been relaxed a little during recent years. It is now possible to obtain an age-related registration number on production of documentation verifying the machine's year of manufacture and proof of purchase. Provided the club or other organisation that authenticates the date of manufacture can supply evidence on their headed notepaper and has the authority of the DVLC to do so, being allocated a registration number should be just a formality. Be sure to obtain a signed receipt from the vendor at the time the sale is completed and check, as far as you can, that the vendor is the machine's legal owner.

Under some circumstances (assuming the registration number has not been re-allocated to another vehicle) it is possible to reclaim it in the UK. An old number plate on which the letters and numbers can still be seen, old tax discs or MOT Test Certificates or better still, old buff or green-coloured log books that confirm the machine's identity will help considerably in this respect.

Irrespective of whatever age and type of machine you buy, and how you find it, we hope these notes will have been of some help to you. May you ride safely and recapture the sense of freedom that only a motorcycle can give, heightened by the knowledge that you are sitting astride a real 'classic'.

CHAPTER FIVE
SELLING A CLASSIC BIKE

Sooner or later you will decide to sell your classic bike, probably in order to acquire another. Quite a few who spend their leisure hours restoring an old motorcycle quickly begin to lose interest when the task is completed. They will have got their enjoyment from converting a derelict wreck or a mass of bits and pieces into a complete machine that is not only usable once again, but also a joy to behold. It is then a case of selling it and starting all over again with something quite different and offering perhaps even a greater challenge! The money-making aspect rarely comes into it; it's the satisfaction of making something from nothing, to put it in a nutshell. Indeed, in a great many cases a sizable loss will have been incurred, as the time taken and its equivalent in labour charges may not have been taken into consideration.

Selling a classic bike may seem a simple task, but there are several different ways of going about this which ought to be taken into consideration. Each has its pitfalls as well as its advantages, so it is as well to be acquainted with them.

What's It Worth?

The first consideration is to decide how much your machine is worth. Looking through the small advertisements in any of the classic motorcycle magazines or newspapers will give an indication of how similar models are priced, although it is not totally reliable. Most prices are subject to negotiation unless otherwise stated, and often are pitched on the high side by the more optimistic vendors, speculating on their value. Dealers in classic motorcycles are likely to sell at higher than average prices (and buy at lower than average!). They are selective in what they buy-in, to safeguard their reputation, and having showrooms to maintain, they have higher overheads. The best guide is probably the price of machines listed in club magazines, where vendors are likely to be closer in estimating their machines' true market value.

Prices, of course, vary according to a number of differing factors, such as whether the machine has some kind of a history, its overall condition, how close it is to its maker's original specification, and whether or not it is a runner. A useful guide to prices, which usually quotes a price range rather than a single figure, appears regularly in a magazine called *Classic Bike Guide*. These prices are based on an analysis of those being asked by private advertisers in their small advertisement columns. Referring to this guide can save you a lot of time, even though not everyone will always agree with any price guide's valuations, and it will leave you to assess exactly where your machine fits into the price range.

Where To Advertise

Having arrived at its valuation, you can now take steps to offer your machine for sale. The most common approach is to advertise it by a small line advertisement in one of the classic motorcycling magazines or newspapers, which one or two such as *Classic Bike Guide* and *British Bike Magazine* will do free of charge. It is as well, however, to have an idea of the circula-

tion figure of each magazine before you decide which one to use. A free of charge advertisement is all very well, but if that magazine has only a small circulation you could be better off taking a paid advertisement in one that sells in much larger numbers. Audit Bureau of Circulation (ABC) figures printed in some of the magazines are an accurate guide in this respect. Advertising in local newspapers is not so effective as only a small percentage of readers will be classic motorcycle enthusiasts. Those that are will, most likely, be looking out for a cheap bargain.

Avoiding Theft

Advertising in this manner does, unfortunately, have its drawbacks these days. There is now a high rate of theft of classic motorcycles, and once you have publicly disclosed your address and/or telephone number, your machine could be on the 'hit' list, no matter how good your security. Many now give only a telephone number in their advertisement, or alternatively, a box number, as a safeguard, although you will lose a large percentage of potentially interested buyers by using a box number rather than your 'phone number, since immediate contact will be lost.

An arrangement should then be made to meet the prospective purchaser away from where the machine is usually kept. If you meet where the machine is kept, the 'purchaser' may appear unimpressed, only to return when least expected and steal it. Be particularly wary if the prospective purchaser wants to try your bike out, itself a perfectly reasonable request. You would be strongly advised to accompany the purchaser on another (modern?) machine. Many classic bikes have been lost when the prospective purchaser offers to leave his own machine as security, only to ride off on yours, never to be seen again! It is only then that you will find the machine he has left has also been stolen! Obviously, in the overwhelming majority of cases, no such things will happen - but it pays to be on your guard!

It goes without saying that you should never accept a cheque until it has been cleared by the bank, which can take up to five days unless you request special (quick) clearance. In rare cases, even Building Society cheques have bounced, because they were either stolen or forgeries. For a quick sale, a banker's draft (which cannot be cancelled) is the obvious answer or better still, hard cash. Obviously it is wise to have the purchaser's name, address and telephone number, along with evidence of identity if you have any worries. Also remember not to part with any of the machine's documents, including the V5 registration document or its equivalent in another country, until ALL the money is safely in your hands (although the V5 document is intrinsically useless, since it is not proof of ownership and replacements can easily be obtained from DVLC).

All this may seem very negative, especially since the vast majority of purchasers will be honest fellow enthusiasts. It is as well to be warned, though, as very few stolen bikes are ever recovered.

The other bugbear in selling by advertising is the time waster, who will take up a disproportionate amount of your time and give the impression that your machine is as good as sold. Remarks such as, "I'll think about it" or, "I'll be around again at the end of the week", are not encouraging signs. The answer to this kind of pest is to request a deposit, and make it clear that otherwise you will sell it to the next person who is interested - and mean it!

An alternative, which often can provide an excellent compromise, is to exchange your machine for the make and model you expect to replace it. All kinds of possibilities are present here, with the addition of cash by either party if there is no parity between the value of the two machines to be swapped. It's probably the best way of ensuring a fair deal all round.

Auctions

1. A quick and convenient way of selling a machine is by auction, although this has its advantages and disadvantages. There will be no disclosure of where your machine is kept, or even of your name, other than to the auctioneer. Furthermore, you will not have to suffer endless telephone calls or visits from prospective purchasers, and will be spared the time wasters. Assuming someone makes a successful bid that either meets or exceeds the reserve figure you place on the machine yourself, it is a quick, clean sale, and the money will be in your hands within a matter of days.

2. Although you will not have to meet any advertising charges, you will have to pay the auctioneer commission on a successful sale, which will cost more. Make sure you know how much this will be before you commit yourself, and whether a seller's premium is likely to be charged over and above this.

3. If you decide to enter your machine for auction, do so in good time, to be sure its details will be included in the auction catalogue. Include two good, clear photos of your machine, one taken from each side, with your auction entry form. Most families have a camera of some kind or other, and 1 hour developing and printing services can be found almost everywhere. Above all else, give as much information as you can on the auction entry form, as this will form the basis of your machine's presentation in the catalogue. Although the more reputable auctioneers employ a consultant to authenticate each entry and originate the catalogue copy, that person cannot make assumptions or check that everything is as it should be from photographs alone. Remember also that it is the quality of the catalogue that will bring in the buyers.

One of the more important keys to a successful sale is pitching the reserve at exactly the right level. Far too many sales are prejudiced by a reserve that is far too high. Although some auctioneers try to overcome this when bids come close to it, it is a ploy that doesn't always work. The only compromise open to them is to say they will sell the machine at a lower figure only with the vendor's approval, after the sale. However, by then the prospective purchaser may well have bought something else, or more than likely is well on his way home! Many a sale has fallen through in this way. Remember, an auctioneer cannot sell below the reserve, which only you can determine. They will always suggest a realistic figure, if asked.

Deal only with a reputable auctioneer, one that specialises in classic motorcycle auctions. To get the best price you need to have the sale handled by professionals who really understand old motorcycles, and not by those more familiar with auctioning furniture or cattle! Only the former are likely to attract a good attendance by classic bike enthusiasts and dealers - and achieve a higher percentage of machines sold at higher prices. Personal recommendations figure highly in selecting the best auctioneer in your part of the country, so don't be afraid to ask around.

One last point, easily forgotten when a deal has been concluded. Don't forget to tear off the bottom portion of the machine's V5 registration document and return it to the DVLC at Swansea after filling in the details. It is a statutory requirement in the UK and may shortly result in a penalty if you fail to do so. Other countries will have their own ruling on this aspect but in almost every transaction the registration authority will have to be notified when change of ownership takes place.

CHAPTER SIX - FAULT FINDING

This Chapter aims to help you to identify and overcome the main faults that are likely to affect either the running or safety aspects of your motorcycle. In the heat of the moment, it is quite easy to overlook a fault that could be corrected quite easily, if the machine's various systems are not checked in a logical sequence. In short, the main requirement is not to panic or leap from one possible cause to another at random. Putting it in its simplest terms, an engine can stop running for only one of three reasons - a mechanical failure, an ignition fault or a fuel system fault. By following the sequences outlined in this Chapter and not taking short cuts you will stand a far better chance of locating the fault and being able to eliminate it. Before carrying out any of the work described in this Chapter, please read carefully *Chapter 1, Safety First!*

Jeff's Law

It is common knowledge that a motorcycle will invariably present problems when it is likely to be needed most, and that if you have two, both will prove unserviceable at the same time!

ENGINE WON'T START

1. Kickstarter won't turn engine over.

2. Kickstarter quadrant jammed in gearbox.

3. Clutch slipping - adjustment or overhaul needed.

4. Engine shaft shock absorber nut has slackened off.

5. Primary chain has broken and snagged in chaincase.

6. Mechanical breakage in engine.

7. Remove plug(s), lay them on bare metal of cylinder head and check for spark when ignition is switched on (coil ignition) and engine is turned over by kickstarter. Do not touch plug(s) or lead(s) during this check.

8. No spark at plug(s).

9. Check plug gap(s) and cleanliness of electrodes. If in doubt, fit new plugs of correct type.

10. Check ignition cut-out and its wiring to ensure neither is shorting out.

11. Is battery discharged? Check whether lighting works.

12. Check switch to ensure ignition is switched on (coil ignition). If magneto ignition, check magneto is rotating as engine is turned over.

13. If points spark regularly as magneto revolves, suspect faulty condenser in magneto armature which will require specialist repair.

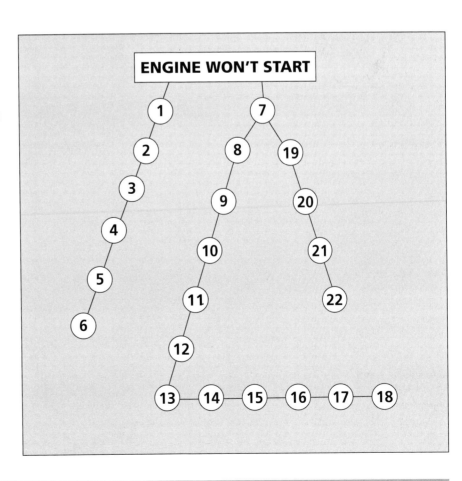

14. Check whether contact breaker points are clean and opening and closing (if coil ignition, with ignition switched OFF). If necessary clean and/or adjust points to correct gap.

15. Switch on ignition and check if contact breaker points spark when separated (coil ignition only). If spark evident, suspect faulty condenser in points circuit.

16. If machine ran before new contact breaker points were fitted they have been assembled incorrectly and a misplaced insulator has immobilised the ignition system.

17. Check whether there is a spark where the HT lead leaves the ignition coil. Check HT lead(s) and sparking plug cap(s) for cracks and clean. Clean also exterior of spark plug(s) If conditions are damp, apply water repellant spray to all exposed parts. Renew any suspect HT lead(s) or cap(s) before spraying.

18. Check ignition circuit wiring for continuity.

19. Visible spark at the plugs.

20. Is the spark weak? Should be an intense blue and not white and hard to see. Faulty condenser (or distributor on multi-cylinder machines) most likely cause.

21. Check that ignition timing has not slipped or has been set incorrectly.

22. Problem with the fuel system. See below.

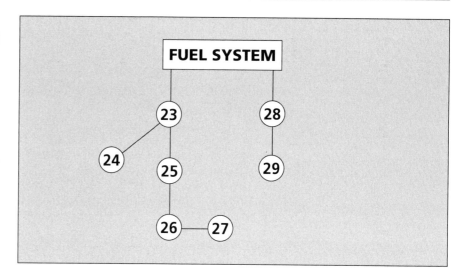

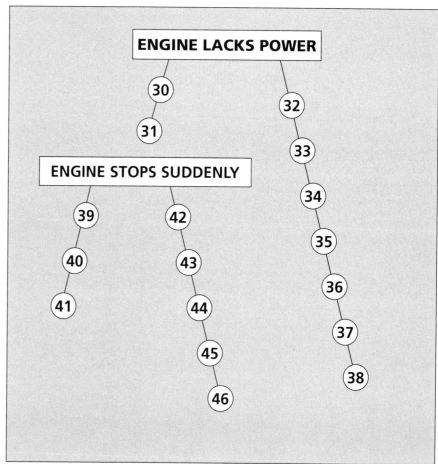

FUEL SYSTEM

23. Detach petrol pipe and check whether petrol (gasoline) flows from tap.

24. If none, check fuel has not run out by switching to reserve. If none still evident, check that breather hole in filler cap is not blocked.

25. If fuel is flowing, check float chamber to see if float is stuck.

26. Check whether engine has become flooded by removing sparking plug(s) and seeing whether electrodes are wet. If so, turn engine over several times before re-fitting plugs and trying again.

27. If no evidence of petrol on spark plug electrode(s) even though carburettor is flooded, suspect blocked main jet. Dismantle and blow jet clear.

28. On any machine, petrol left during long storage may have deteriorated, as evidenced by distinctive 'stale' smell. Drain off and refill with fresh petrol.

29. If a two-stroke that has been left standing for a long while, drain float chamber and refill with petrol/oil mix. Petrol may have evaporated during storage, leaving only the oil content.

ENGINE LACKS POWER

30. Lack of oil is causing engine to tighten up. Stop engine immediately and check engine oil content (four-strokes only).

31. Incorrect ratio of oil to petrol is causing engine to tighten up. (two-strokes only).

32. Valve clearances set incorrectly or have closed up. Stop engine and re-set clearances when engine is cold (unless otherwise stated by manufacturer).

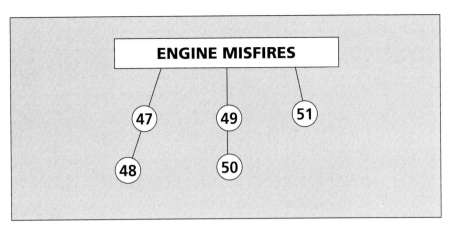

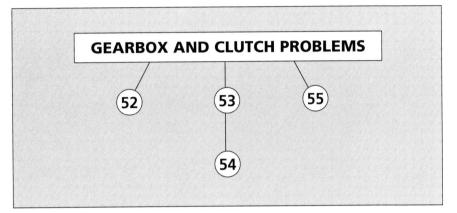

44. Ignition cut-out shorted to earth (ground).

45. Contact breaker return spring broken.

46. Magneto drive failed causing ignition timing to slip.

ENGINE MISFIRES

47. Dirt or water in petrol (gasoline) obstructing or partly obstructing carburettor jets. Drain petrol tank, clean carburettor jets and refill with new petrol.

48. Stale petrol resulting from long storage. Can usually be identified by distinctive smell. Drain petrol tank, clean carburettor, and refill.

49. Backfire when engine is on over-run. Air leak in exhaust system.

50. If ignition timing over-retarded, engine will overheat and appear sluggish and could also backfire on over-run.

51. If ignition timing over-advanced, will kick back when kickstarted and run roughly except at high speeds. Re-set to recommended setting.

33. Engine will run only when carburettor is flooded. Worn or damaged oil seals allowing air to leak into crankcase. Strip engine and renew seals (two-strokes only).

34. Leakage of coolant is causing engine to tighten up. Stop engine immediately and allow to cool before checking radiator and all hose connections.

35. Air filter has been removed without increasing size of main jet to compensate.

36. Ignition timing has become retarded. Re-set to recommended setting.

37. Blocked silencer. Remove baffles, clean and replace. Check also whether exhaust ports have heavy carbon build-up (two-strokes only).

38. Brakes binding. Raise machine off the ground and check that both wheels spin freely. Warm or hot brake plate, or brake disc, will confirm brakes are rubbing.

ENGINE STOPS SUDDENLY

39. No electrical power available.

40. Broken or earthed (grounded) electrical connection (coil ignition).

41. Battery fully discharged (coil ignition only).

42. Electrical power available to other components.

43. Defective or whiskered sparking plug (unlikely to cause a multi cylinder engine to stop dead).

GEARBOX AND CLUTCH PROBLEMS

52. Gearbox jumps out of gear. Worn gear selector or dogs on the ends of the gear pinions in mesh when this happens. Renew all worn parts (specialist attention).

53. Difficulty in finding neutral when stopped. Dragging clutch. Re-adjust, keeping small amount of slack in operating cable.

FUEL SYSTEM - SAFETY FIRST!
*Before working on the fuel system, read **Chapter 1, Safety First!** Take special care to 1) only work out of doors; 2) wear suitable gloves and goggles and keep fuel out of eyes and away from skin: it is known to be carcinogenic; 3) if fuel does come into contact with skin, wash off straight away; 4) if fuel gets into your eyes, wash out with copious amounts of clean, cold water. Seek medical advice if necessary; 5) when draining fuel or testing for fuel flow, drain or pump into a sufficiently large container, minimising splashes; 6) don't smoke, work near flames or sparks or work when the engine or exhaust are hot.*

54. Difficulty in selecting gears. Dragging clutch or gear selector, or indexing mechanism at fault. Specialist attention required.

55. Machine does not move faster as engine speed increases. Slipping clutch. Re-adjust clutch and check free movement in handlebar lever before lever starts to disengage clutch. Check linings for wear.

LIGHTING PROBLEMS

56. Lights fail completely.

57. Break in main lead from battery or battery's earth (ground) connection. (Note: Very few motorcycles manufactured during the period covered by this book were fitted with fuses).

58. Lights are dim.

59. Poor earth (ground) return in main lighting connection.

60. Lights flicker constantly.

61. Damaged insulation in wiring causing short circuits.

62. Dynamo or alternator not charging battery.

63. Check for stripped teeth on fibre pinion driving dynamo. (Lucas Magdyno only.)

64. Intermittent charge from dynamo or alternator.

65. Badly adjusted voltage regulator unit (DC systems only.) Adjustment of the regulator requires professional attention.

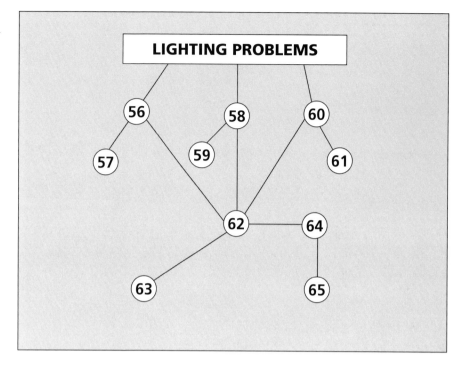

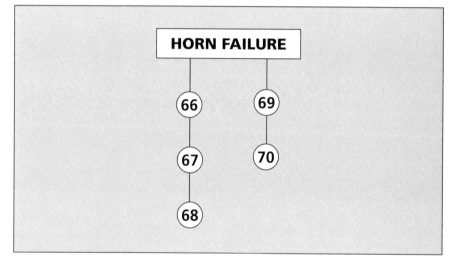

HORN FAILURE

66. Horn will not sound.

67. Break in wire from horn button to power supply from battery.

68. Horn out of adjustment. Limited means of adjustment accessible on horn body.

69. Horn will not stop sounding.

70. Short inside horn button causing it to earth (ground).

CHAPTER SEVEN
GETTING THROUGH THE MOT

Getting your classic bike through its annual MOT Test always gives rise to concern, rather like a visit to a dentist when you have not set foot in the surgery for a while. Yet if you think about it carefully, and your motorcycle has been looked after in the way outlined in this book, the chances are that you have no cause to worry at all.

Any motorcycle more than three years old has to go through the MOT Test annually so that its owner can present a valid test certificate to show it has passed, whenever the machine is taxed for use on the road. In some respects the test is now something of a misnomer as it has for some time been the DOT Test. When the statutory requirement to have a motorised vehicle tested came into effect in 1961, the responsibility then rested with the Ministry of Transport. Now it rests with the Department of Transport.

Part 1: MOT Test Checks

The information that follows applies only to motorcycles used in the UK although UK owners should also check the latest regulations for themselves. Other countries may well have their own requirements that need to be met by elderly motorcycles.

If this book is used outside the UK it is advisable to acquaint yourself with whatever special regulations apply (if any) in the country where you will be using your machine. IMPORTANT NOTE: UK regulations are also regularly modified. Check them out with your local MOT Testing Station.

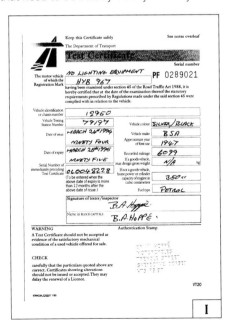

I. To put the mind of UK readers at rest, any fully roadworthy motorcycle should pass the test with ease and this is what you'll be presented with as and when your machine passes. The MOT test has been devised to ensure all vehicles meet basic safety requirements and not that they are in virtually 'as new' condition. Allowances are made for general wear and tear within certain limits, and in the case of older machines, special dispensation is given to compensate for the lower standard of braking performance expected from drum brakes. Special allowance is also made for competition models that have no lighting equipment by exempting them from the lighting checks that would otherwise have been made during the test.

Preparing Your Machine For The Test

It is a sensible precaution to give your machine a thorough check before the date of the test, to ensure it is not likely to fail as the result of a minor fault that has been overlooked. It will also help considerably by creating a good first impression if you present a clean, well-maintained machine to the tester. The majority of classic bike owners will not need to be reminded of this, because invariably they take pride in keeping their machine(s) in this condition. It goes without saying that a dirty and scruffy machine will not only suggest its owner knows or cares little about regular routine maintenance, but also is seemingly unaware of the potential danger of running it in a neglected condition. On a machine such as this, the tester is likely to have a field day!

If the machine has not been used for a couple of weeks or more since its last service, it is a good idea to carry out at least the *Daily (before-use) Check* as described in Chapter 3, before you set off for the test. It will help to make you aware of any areas where further attention is likely to be needed.

Make sure the machine has plenty of petrol (gasoline) and oil to get you to and from the test and that the machine displays a valid tax disc.

If it is untaxed, as may well be the case if a full-scale restoration has just been completed, it is still permissible to ride it to and from a testing station if you have first booked a firm appointment. You must ride it the most direct way there, and back home again - going for a long ride after it has passed is not acceptable if your bike does not display a valid tax disc. It follows, of course, that the machine must be fully insured to meet the requirements of the Road Traffic Act, no matter under what circumstances it is taken on to the road.

Put To The Test

On arrival, the first check will be of the engine and frame numbers, so be sure you know where they are. If the frame number is obscured by paint, carefully chip it away beforehand so that the number and any prefix or suffix letters can be easily checked. After this formality all the following checks will be carried out, not necessarily in the order given below:

1. The condition of the controls, control cables, switches, horn and cut-out buttons on the handlebars. A brake lever that touches the handlebars before the brake is fully applied will result in a test failure, as will frayed control cables or those with cracks or other damage to their outer cover. The controls must be clamped securely to the handlebars.

2. The handlebars, for security of mounting. The adjustment of the steering head bearings will also be checked. The handlebars must turn freely from lock to lock, without trapping cables or being restricted by them. There must be no play or judder at the steering head bearings when the front brake is applied hard while the machine is being wheeled along.

3. The front fork, to ensure it is in line and moves freely. If the fork is damped, its damping action will be checked. Any significant wear in the fork bushes found by pulling and pushing the lower fork legs (sliders) will result in a test failure, as will evidence of oil leaks.

4. The rear suspension and the pivoted rear fork for signs of excessive wear or restricted movement. The rear suspension units fitted to a pivoted fork system or a Earles-type front fork should show evidence of damping when the suspension is depressed. Oil leaks are not acceptable. Worn bushes in the pivoted rear fork or plunger-type rear suspension units will cause the machine to fail the test as they will affect its handling.

5. The front wheel and its bearings. The machine will have its front end raised off the ground so that the wheel can be spun to ensure it revolves quite freely and that the brakes are not binding. The wheel bearings will be checked for any play at the same time.

6. The rear wheel and its bearings. By placing the machine on its rear or centre stand, a similar check will be carried out on the rear wheel.

7. Proceeding along the right-hand side of the machine, the frame will be checked for signs of damage or corrosion and security of mounting of the mudguards, seat, footrests and exhaust system. The last mentioned must be in good condition and free from any holes or splits. Repairs are acceptable but only if of a permanent nature. Note that there is no specific recommendation about exhaust noise. At the time of writing this is left to the tester's discretion. If the exhaust is considered too noisy, or if it smokes excessively, the tester is within his rights to fail the machine. Currently, there is no exhaust emission test as far as motorcycles are concerned.

8. At the rear of the machine the operation of the stop and tail lamp will be tested, and also the turn signal lights, if fitted. A check will also be made to ensure a separate, undamaged reflector is fitted, even if one is incorporated in the rear lamp lens.

9. A similar check to item 7 will be made along the left-hand side of the machine, looking for loose fittings and making sure the rear brake pedal moves freely without excessive play in its pivot.

10. The headlamp, to ensure the main bulb operates in both main and dipped beam positions, and that the pilot lamp works. The reflector must not be discoloured or have its coating peeling off. The headlamp glass must not be cracked and the whole assembly must be securely mounted. It will then be checked for correct alignment in both the main and dipped beam positions.

10a. You can't match the accuracy of an MOT station's beam setter, but you can get things roughly right with your bike 25 feet away from a wall, on level ground - best done at night. (See illustration 1 on page 110.)

10b. The headlamp mountings adjust the vertical aim; adjust the focus by slackening the clamp and moving the bulb until you have a uniform beam without a dark centre. (See illustration 2 on page 110, early models only.)

11. With the machine raised on its stand, the wheels will be checked for alignment. The wheel rims must run true and have no dents or flats, nor must there be any rusty, loose or broken spokes. Repairs to alloy wheels or rims are not acceptable. The tyres will be inspected for general wear and tear at the same time and also for any imperfections in either the sidewalls or the tread. Uneven wear will necessitate a closer look at the machine to ascertain how it has been caused. The following are some of the more common causes of tyre failure that will result in a motorcycle failing the test:

a) Lumps and bulges in the sidewalls of a tyre. These usually result from accidental damage such as striking a kerb or occasionally from a defect during the manufacture of the tyre. In either case the tyre should not be used. Often, when it is removed from the wheel rim, the cause of the problem will be more obvious from the inside of its carcass.

b) Abrasion of the sidewall. This can also occur as the result of striking a kerb, but more likely from doing so obliquely and running along it. It can also result from striking a pothole in the road. To continue to run a tyre in this condition is also dangerous and it should be replaced without question.

c) Some signs of cracking on the sidewalls may well be found, mostly only superficial in nature as the result of exposure to sunlight and a normal aging process. With tyres, it always pays to play safe, so even if the tyre passed the test, renew it rather than continue to use it in this condition.

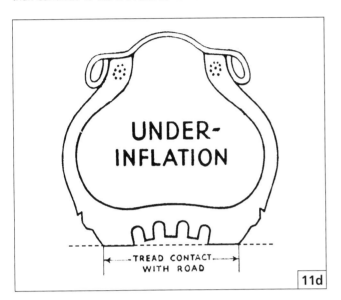

11d

d) If the outer edges of the tyre have worn more rapidly than the centre, this is a sure sign the tyre has been run under-inflated. Apart from being illegal to do so, it is also dangerous and will affect the machine's handling.

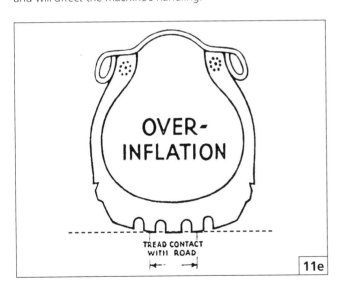

11e

e) If the centre of the tyre tread has worn more noticeably than the outer edges, the tyre has been run over-inflated. This too is illegal and will have a similar adverse effect on the machine's handling. Always run your machine's tyres at the recommended pressure and increase the pressure in the rear tyre by the specified amount if you carry a pillion passenger.

f) If the tread has worn more on one side of a tyre than on the other, this is invariably due to either a bent frame and/or front

fork, or the wheels being out of line. It is a condition that needs to be corrected immediately as the machine cannot possibly handle satisfactorily under these circumstances.

g) The tread depth must not be less than 1mm over three quarters of the tread breadth around the tyre's entire circumference. Obviously and motorcyclist is ill advised to let either tyre wear to this extent, when its replacement becomes a statutory requirement. By then there will have been a marked deterioration in wet grip, even though it not have been noticed as the rate of wear will have taken place at a very low rate. We strongly recommend replacing a tyre when there is an absolute minimum of 2mm of tread left as described above and preferably more if the machine is in constant use or is to be used for a long journey.

12. The brakes. They will be tested, either by means of a static brake tester or a rolling road. The former is attached to the machine, which is then winched forward by means of a cable attached to a gauge while the brake being tested is fully applied. A reading will be taken when the strength of the pull is sufficient to overcome the locked wheel and cause it to start to revolve.

13. The number plates. A change in legal requirements means that a motorcycle now needs only to have a rear number plate. However, many classic motorcycles also have a front number plate fitted, in recognition that this was also a legal requirement at the time when the machine was first manufactured. The traditional white numbers on a black background, front and rear, are acceptable for most machines manufactured during the period covered by this book. Reflective number plates did not become an obligatory fitting except for all machines that were first registered on or after 1st January 1973. The letters and numbers must be of the correct size and spacing and not be closed to make up words or written in 'computer' style format.

14. If a sidecar is fitted, additional checks will be made on the sidecar and its fittings. These will relate to the sidecar's wheel, tyre, brake (if fitted) and its suspension system. Its attachment points and their arrangement will also receive attention, as will the swivel joints on any sidecars of the 'banking' type. Note that a sidecar must be fitted with two rear lamps and two reflectors. The rear lamps must be of the same appearance when illuminated and must be wired in parallel so that if one fails, the other is unaffected. The reflectors must be mounted at the same height.

The alignment of the sidecar in relation to the motorcycle will also be taken into account. A badly aligned sidecar can have a marked effect on how the whole outfit will handle.

15. A competition machine that has no lights will be exempt from the lighting requirements of the test provided there is no evidence of lighting equipment such as a headlamp, tail lamp or any lighting circuit wiring. A Lucas Magdyno or similar will be acceptable provided the dynamo is isolated and is not connected up with any electrical wiring. Competition machines with no lighting can be used legally only during the hours of daylight and must carry a rear-mounted reflector and also a audible warning of approach such as a bulb horn.

Part II: DIY for the MOT

Checking Headlamp Alignment

Unlike cars, it is relatively easy to realign a motorcycle head-lamp by slackening its mounting bolts and moving it in the desired direction before re-tightening them. The following procedure is suggested:

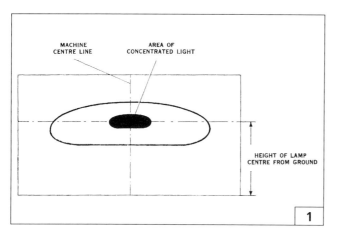

1. Position the machine on level ground having a flat wall at one end on to which the light can be directed. Draw a line at right angles to the wall so that the machine can be located perpendicular to the wall surface. If the line is continued up the wall for some four feet or so, this can be used as the target for aligning the light after positioning the machine so that the front of the headlamp is 25 feet from the wall. (Illustration, courtesy Lucas)

Sit someone astride the machine (standing on its own wheels and not on a centre or rear stand) in the normal riding position and measure the height of the centre of the headlamp from the ground. Draw a horizontal line on the wall at this height, to bisect the vertical line already drawn.

Check the motorcycle is correct located along the line drawn at a right angle to the wall and turn on the light in the main beam position. The centre spot of the beam should be exactly where the vertical and horizontal lines intersect. Make adjustments by slackening the headlamp retaining bolts and moving the headlamp to the correct position. Check the position has not altered after the bolts have been re-tightened.

2. Adjust the focus so that the beam is uniform with no dark centre by slackening the clamp and moving the bulb in or out - appropriate models only.

The headlamp on European and American specification machines may have what is known as an asymmetric dipped beam arrangement. This means the area of maximum brightness should be to the left of the vertical line and just below the horizontal line, when in the dipped beam position.

From the foregoing it will be realised that the way in which the

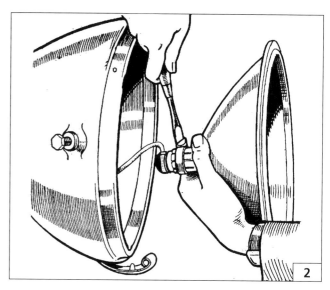

various requirements of the test are interpreted will depend at times on the tester's own point of view. Training will have been given by the Department of Transport to serve as a guide when having to make decisions, followed by regular update courses from time to time. If a machine is failed, it can be re-presented within a specified period of time, in which case the full test fee will not have to be paid. If the owner feels he has been unjustly treated, there is a recognised complaint procedure which he or she can follow to get the matter resolved.

Full details of the MOT Test and all the requirements that have to be fulfilled in order to pass can be found in an HMSO Publication entitled "The MOT Inspection Manual, Motor Cycle Testing". Some regard it as advantageous to keep all the old certificates as part of the machine's history, which can prove helpful whenever it is sold, as they have mileage readings incorporated.

Removing and Fitting Tyres

3. At some time or other you will need to remove and fit tyres, either as the result of a puncture or because they have worn to the extent that a replacement is needed. Many motorcyclists seem to regard this as a difficult task, to be performed only with reluctance. Yet if the job is tackled systematically, it is really quite easy. The following technique, which applies to tubed tyres only, should help considerably in removing any such unwarranted anxieties, even to the most inexperienced. Brute force should NEVER be needed.

Removing a Tyre

a) Remove the wheel from the machine and lay it flat on a clean surface. Unscrew the valve cap, remove the rim nut and valve core, and allow the inner tube to deflate.

b) Push the bead on each side of the tyre off the shoulder of the wheel rim, towards the well in the wheel's centre.

c) Push the tyre valve in as far as it will go, then insert a tyre

3c

lever at a point diametrically opposite the valve. Use it to lift the bead over the wheel rim.

d) Hold the lever firmly with one hand and insert another tyre

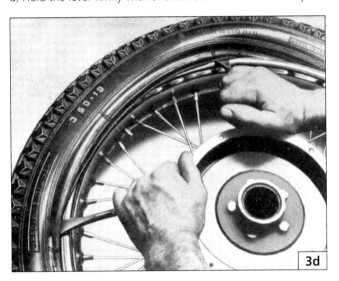

3d

lever a short distance away. Use it to lift a further portion of the tyre bead over the wheel rim.

e) Continue in this fashion in easy stages until the whole of the

3e

tyre bead on that side has lifted off the wheel rim. Withdraw the inner tube, starting from the side opposite the valve. When the inner tube has been removed, lever the bead off the other

side of the wheel rim and remove the tyre completely.

Fitting a Tyre

f) First check that the tyre, tube and rim tape are sound. DO NOT use insulating tape as a substitute for the latter. Make sure there is no grit, foreign matter or wrapping paper inside the tyre, which will otherwise cause damage.

g) Inflate the inner tube sufficiently for it to become completely round, then slide it into the tyre. This is made easier if the tube is first lightly dusted with french chalk. Make sure the tube is not creased or twisted.

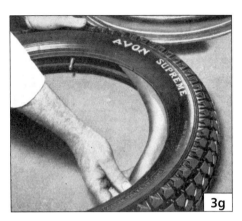

3g

h) Lightly lubricate the lower edge of each tyre bead, using either french chalk or the special tyre soap used by tyre fitters. DO NOT use either ordinary soap or washing up liquid. Both will cause the wheel rim to corrode and rust, particularly as the latter contains salt.

i) Lay the tyre with its tube inside on top of the wheel, with the valve in line with the valve hole in the rim. The direction of rotation of the tyre is often important, and will be marked clearly on the tyre wall. The tread direction on front and rear tyres may be quite different.

3j

j) With the inner tube still in the tyre, thread the valve through the valve hole and temporarily secure it with its rim nut on the first few threads only. Allow the lower tyre bead to sink into the well of the wheel rim, and the upper rim to remain on the outside of the rim. Remove the valve core and allow the inner tube to deflate.

3k

k) Working from each side of the valve, and using both hands, press the remainder of the lower bead over the rim, using a tyre lever if necessary. The bead area diametrically opposite the point of fitting must always be in the well of the wheel rim to make this possible without having to use excessive force. Take care not to trap and puncture the inner tube (easily done!).

3l

l) Fit the second bead in a similar manner, starting diametrically opposite the valve. As before, make sure the bead is in the well of the rim as the tyre is fitted and work round in both directions until only a small portion of the unfitted bead remains in the vicinity of the valve.

3m

m) It should then be gently levered into position while depressing the valve slightly. Make sure the inner tube is not trapped close to the valve by pushing inwards before pulling it finally back into position and tightening the rim nut.

n) Make sure the tyre has been fitted evenly all round so that the line moulded in the sidewall is equidistant from the wheel rim on both sides. The valve must protrude squarely through the valve hole and not at an angle, otherwise it is likely to get ripped out when the wheel revolves. When you have verified everything is correct, inflate the tyre to the correct pressure and check again that the line moulded in the sidewalls is equidistant from the wheel rim on both sides.

o) Do not use excessive force when trying to get a tyre off or on to a wheel rim. If this proves necessary, it is a sure sign that the bead of the tyre opposite where it is being removed or refitted is not in the well in the centre of the wheel rim. If you continue to use excessive force, the tyre and especially its beads will be damaged irreparably.

p) To avoid the tyre levers damaging a wheel rim during tyre removal or refitting, especially if it is an alloy or a painted rim, use rim flange protectors.

COMPETITION MODELS: WHEELS WITH SECURITY BOLTS

q) Competition models often have wheels fitted with one or two security bolts, used to keep the tyre firmly on the rim when it is run at very low pressures. When removing a tyre,

3q

slacken off and remove the nut and washers that retain the security bolt and push it into the tyre when prising off the bead in that area.

r) When fitting a tyre, fit the security bolt(s) before the inner tube valve is pushed through the valve hole and retain it (them) in position by having the washers and the securing nut at the very end of the thread. The security bolt(s) can then be pushed into the tyre as the bead is fitted on either side. When the tyre is on the rim completely, check that the inner tube sits on the security bolt(s) flap and is not trapped under it. Tighten up the securing nut(s) only when the tyre has been inflated to its correct pressure. One security bolt should be 9 in. in front of the tyre valve when the wheel is rotated in its usual direction.

3r

CHAPTER EIGHT
TOOLS AND EQUIPMENT

Basic maintenance on any classic motorcycle can be carried out using a fairly simple and relatively inexpensive tool kit. There is no need to spend a fortune on getting together a really comprehensive set of tools and equipment as in practice most owners who carry out their own servicing manage to build this up over a period of time. Even so, while we have concentrated on those items necessary to keep your machine on the road and running sweetly, we have included some additional 'nice to have' items which will help make servicing that much easier and more professional.

One vital point - always buy the best quality tools you can afford. Cheap items of unknown origin may look similar to their more expensive counterparts, but experience shows they often fail, sometimes with dangerous consequences. If looked after properly and not abused, good quality tools will last a lifetime and can be regarded as an investment. In the long run the money will prove well spent.

Bear in mind that if your propose to keep your motorcycle for some time some of the special service tools made for it could be worth looking at. They will make the removal and replacement of parts that require regular attention very much easier and will do so with less risk of damage to them. Even if the factory originals are no longer available, quite a few pattern service tools are available that will give equally good service. Service tools are especially useful in pulling off parts that are a tight fit and which may otherwise prove very difficult to dislodge.

The following lists are shown under headings which indicate the type of use for which each group of tools and piece of equipment are best suited.

hydraulic workbench, with which the machine can be raised off the ground to a more comfortable working level. Crouching beside the machine or even lying alongside it to gain access to some inaccessible part is hardly a comfortable position to be in, the more so as that is where all the draughts will be found! With the machine at a reasonable working level it is far less tiring and more relaxing - and there can be little doubt that the older owner will find it particularly beneficial.

A. There are several different makes of workbench on the market at present, the more expensive of which have their own hydraulic unit. The cheaper versions rely on the use of a separate car trolley jack or a winch for raising and lowering, the bench. (Illustration, courtesy A.R.E. Ltd.)

If you decide to invest in a workbench, make sure its maximum safe loading comfortably exceeds the overall weight of your machine plus all its accessories and fuel and oil. Also be sure that when it is in the raised position there is no possibility of it inadvertently being lowered and that the rate at which it can be lowered can be controlled. The consequences of a workbench collapsing without warning are too dreadful to contemplate.

Lifting:

Unlike a car, there is no necessity to work on the underside of a motorcycle as virtually every job can be carried out from either side. However, it is worth serious consideration to buy an

Thread Types:

INSIDE INFORMATION: Classic bikes are renowned for having a remarkable number of fasteners with different thread format and sizes. It is quite common to find British Standard Cycle (formerly

CEI), British Standard Whitworth (BSW), British Standard Fine (BSF), British Association (BA) all on the one machine! And that does not take into account the British Standard Pipe thread used for many petrol and oil tank fittings, and sparking plugs, which have their own thread size. Later machines are likely to have mostly A/F or UNC thread sizes of American origin, and if of Continental manufacture, Metric sizes. A set of thread gauges is clearly a handy item to have if you are unsure of what threads are employed on your own machine!

Spanners:

B. A set of open-ended spanners is an essential purchase, possibly accompanied by a set of ring spanners. The latter will give a more positive grip on a bolt head or nut, assuming access with sufficient clearance is not a problem. As a starting point, the combination spanners illustrated would be ideal.

C. Socket spanners can also be very useful in a confined space, as they can be used in conjunction with a ratchet handle or a long extension bar. A set of Allen keys should complete the ensemble of spanners; if you own an old British bike, make sure you don't purchase a set of metric keys in error!

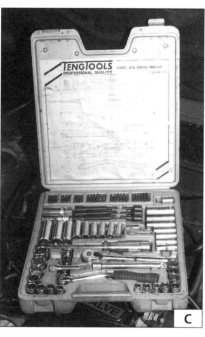

D. An adjustable spanner is a worth while addition, as inevitably there will be an awkward size nut that none of your other spanners will fit.

E. A sparking plug spanner is also an essential requirement, preferably one fitted with a rubber 'plug grip' insert that will retain a hot plug after it has been unscrewed. One with a ratchet handle is the best buy, although the 'T' bar type can also be used, though sometimes less conveniently.

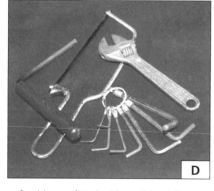

F. Although a torque wrench tends to be a very useful tool to make sure fasteners are tightened the correct amount, they are superfluous for most British-made motorcycles. Few manufacturers gave the recommended torque figure setting in their handbooks or instruction manuals except in later years.

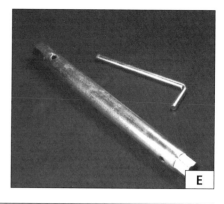

Screwdrivers:

G. A good set of general purpose flat blade and cross head sizes makes a wise investment.

An impact driver is also exceptionally useful for removing screws that are either seized or very tight. It will come with a variety of flat

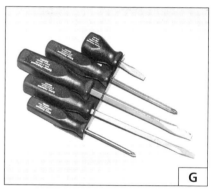

bladed and cross headed bits to suit most sizes. Make sure you purchase a well-known brand. There have been many cases where the bits have twisted out of all recognition or have even shattered on impact due either to lack of hardening or the wrong materials.

'Tuning' Aids:

Depending on how much of the servicing you wish to carry out yourself, you'll need all of the following items.

Compression gauge, preferably the screw-in rather than the push-in type.

INSIDE INFORMATION: Note that manufacturers of the older machines rarely quoted a figure for the compression in a cylinder. Consult your specialist or club for advice on your particular model.

Set of feeler gauges.

Sparking plug gap adjuster tool (safer to use than bending the outer electrode with a screwdriver).

H. Xenon stroboscopic timing light (neon types can be used but the less

intense light makes them more difficult to use). Applicable for use only on the later classic bikes provided with timing marks). Carburettor balancing/adjusting tool. Applicable only to the later, multi-cylinder models. Colortune. A means of enabling you to view the colour of the spark as you adjust the carburettor settings

Degree disc or dial gauge. Useful for determining when the piston is exactly at top dead centre when checking or re-setting the ignition timing.

Sundry Items For The Workshop:

A tool box - preferably of the lockable steel type.
Extension lead.
Inspection lamp.
Small/ medium size ball pein hammer.
Soft ended mallet.
Brass bristle wire brush for cleaning sparking plugs.
Copper-based anti-seize compound - useful during the assembly of threaded components that will subsequently be subjected to heat.
Gasket cement.
Grease gun.
Oil can (filled with 15W/50 oil for general lubrication).
Water dispellant aerosol spray.
Contact cleaner aerosol spray.
Pair of standard jaw pliers.
Pair of long nosed (snipe ended) pliers.
Pair of side cutters.
Self-grip wrench.
Junior hacksaw.
Stud removing tools (nice to have when a stud shears off flush).
Tyre pump.
Tyre pressure gauge.
Tyre thread depth gauge.
Drifts - a set can prove extremely useful as a 'nice to have' item.
An adjustable sprocket puller with thin ended jaws.
Electrical test meter.
6/12 volt test lamp (can be made up using crocodile clips)
6/12 volt battery charger.
Centre punch.
Electric drill.

I. The last two items are not, strictly speaking, service tools, although they are a virtual necessity. A rechargeable electric drill is preferable, not only as it is safer to use out of doors, avoiding the risk of electric

shock, but also as it can be used to get at restricted areas where a trailing lead might prove inconvenient.

Tool Kit For The Bike:

Only too often motorcyclists today venture out, often for quite long journeys, without carrying a single tool in the machine's toolbox. While admittedly the later classic motorcycles have a much

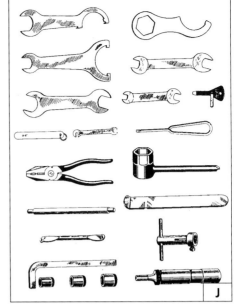

higher standard of reliability than their predecessors, roadside breakdowns are still likely to occur. Invariably this is bound to happen at the most inconvenient time, under inhospitable conditions, and where there are no repair facilities within easy reach.

J. Much of this kind of problem can be overcome if a basic tool kit to deal with most of the more common emergencies is carried in the machine's toolbox. You may not have the 'original' tool kit shown here: indeed, you may not want to carry it with you all the time if you have! Putting together a kit comprising the following items could save you a long walk:

A complete set of open-ended spanners.
A screwdriver.
A pair of pliers
A spare spring link to fit each of the chains.
A spare clutch and throttle cable.
Solderless nipples to fit each size of control cable fitted.
A puncture repair outfit.
A tyre pressure gauge.
A motorcycle tyre pump (fitted on the machine).
A spare tyre valve cap.
A pair of tyre levers.
A small roll of wire (plain and insulated).
A selection of nuts and bolts in a tin.
A spare sparking plug.
A plug spanner.
A spare set of contact breaker points.

All the tools listed above can be packed into a tool roll, as originally would have been supplied when the machine was new. The tool roll can then be wrapped up with the puncture outfit and the other oddments in a large piece of cloth secured with rubber bands cut from an old inner tube. For safety's sake, the sparking plug should have a protective end cap fitted to protect the electrodes. The cloth can be used to clean any parts before fitting them, and then the hands after the bike is ready to take to the road again.

The tool kit should be kept as compact as possible, not only so that it can fit within the toolbox but also so that it can be carried around if the machine is parked in an unguarded area. Sadly, a tool kit is just as likely to be stolen as the bike itself in these days when the incidence of theft is high.

APPENDIX 1
RECOMMENDED CASTROL LUBRICANTS
for classic motorcycles (two-strokes and four-strokes)

	APPLICATION	REQUIREMENTS	OLD CASTROL GRADE	PRESENT DAY RECOMMENDATION
1.	**Engine**	4 stroke engines	Castrol XL	Castrol Classic XL 30
		2 stroke engines	Castrol Two-Stroke Self Mixing Oil	Castrol Supper TT
2.	**Gearbox**	Semi-fluid grease	Castrolease Medium	Castrol DK Grease Castrol Impervia TR Light Castrol Impervia MMO
		Monograde SAE 30 engine oil	Castrol XL	Castrol Classic XL 30
		Monograde SAE 40 engine oil	Castrol XXL	Castrol Product 351
		Multigrade SAE 10W/40 engine oil	Castrolite	Castrol MTX
		Non extreme pressure SAE 90 gear oil	Castrol ST	Castrol ST 90 Castrol Classic GP 50
		Non extreme pressure SAE 140 gear oil	Castrol D	Castrol Hi-Press EP 140
		Extreme pressure SAE 80W gear oil		Castrol Hypoy Light EP 80W
		Extreme pressure SAE 90 gear oil	Castrol Hypoy	Castrol Hypoy EP 90
		Extreme pressure SAE 140 gear oil	Castrol Hi-press	Castrol Hi-Press EP 140
3.	**Primary Chain Case**	Monograde SAE 30 engine oil	Castrol XL	Castrol Classic XL 30
4.5.6.7.	**Grease Points**	General Greasing	Castrolease Heavy	Castrol LM Grease
		Chassis lubrication	Castrolease LM	
		Wheel bearings		
8.9.	**Dynamo & exposed cables, all brake rod joints & pins**	Thin lubricating oil		Castrol Everyman Oil
	Brake Fluid (Where applicable)	FMVSS DOT 3 & 4	Castrol Girling Crimson	Castrol Universal Brake & Clutch Fluid
	External Chain	Chain lubrication		Castrol Chain Spray

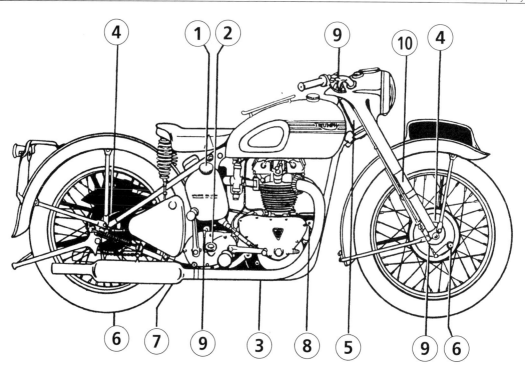

APPENDIX 2
AMERICAN AND BRITISH TERMS

It was Mark Twain who described the British and the Americans as "two nations divided by a common language". While such cynicism has no place here, we do acknowledge that our common language has diversified into different directions. We hope the following glossary of terms, commonly encountered when servicing your classic motorcycle, will be of assistance to American enthusiasts and, in some cases, English speaking owners in other parts of the world too.

American	British
Air cleaner	Air filter
Axle	Spindle
Bash plate	Crankcase shield
Boot	Gaiter
Bushing	Bush
Carburetor	Carburettor
Snap ring	Circlip
Counterclockwise	Anticlockwise
Cotter pin	Split pin
Countershaft	Layshaft
Drive train	Transmission
Fender	Mudguard
Footpeg	Footrest
Gasoline	Petrol
Frozen	Seized
Ground (electrical)	Earth (electrical)
Header	Exhaust pipe
Input shaft	Mainshaft
Intake	Inlet
Kerosene	Paraffin
Kick stand	Prop stand
License plate	Number plate
Muffler	Silencer
Petcock	Petrol tap
Pinging	Pinking
Shift lever	Gear change pedal
Shifter	Selector
Shock	Shock absorber/ suspension unit

American	British
Side cases	Panniers
Tab washer	Lock washer
Throw-out bearing	Thrust bearing
Tire iron	Tyre lever
Valve cotters	Valve collets
Valve lifter	Cam follower
Vise grips	Self-locking pliers
Wrench	Spanner
Wrist or piston pin	Gudgeon pin

Useful Conversion Factors

	Multiply by
US gallons to litres	3.785
Litres to US gallons	0.2642
UK gallons to US gallons	1.20095
US gallons to UK gallons	0.832674

Fahrenheit to Celsius (Centigrade)

Subtract 32 and multiply by 0.5555

Celsius to Fahrenheit

Multiply by 1.8 and add 32

SPECIALISTS & SUPPLIERS

APPENDIX 3
SPECIALISTS AND SUPPLIERS
FEATURED IN THIS BOOK

All of the products and services listed below have contributed in various ways to this book or have been used personally by the author to his complete satisfaction. The consumer products are available through regular high street outlets.

A.R.E. Ltd, East Street, Farnham, Surrey GU9 7XU
Tel: 01252 711777
Suppliers of hydraulic workbenches.

Avon Tyres Limited, Bath Road, Melksham, Wiltshire, SN12 8AA Tel: 01225 703101
Manufacturers of Avon motorcycle tyres in both modern and classic patterns and sizes.

Castrol (UK) Ltd, Burmah House, Pipers Way, Swindon, Wiltshire, SN3 1RE. Tel: 01793 452222
Contact Castrol's Consumer Technical Department Help Line on the above number for assistance with lubrication recommendations.

Dave Booth, 36 Pagham Close, Mill Reach, Emsworth, Hants. PO18 8JB. Tel: 01243 378447
Speedometer and tachometer repairs of all kinds.

Robin James Engineering Ltd., Clinton Road, Leominster, Hereford, HE6 0RJ. Tel: 01568 612800
Classic motorcycle restoration and repair services.

Gunson Ltd, Coppen Road, Dagenham, Essex, RM8 1NU. Tel: 0181 984 8853
Electrical and electronic engine tuning equipment.

Kamasa Tools, Saxon Industries, Lower Everland Road, Hungerford, Berkshire, RG17 0DX
Wide range of hand and power tools, used throughout this book.

Mail Spares, The Firs, Othery, Somerset, TA7 0QS. Tel: 01823 698305
Suppliers of vintage and classic motorcycle spares and accessories.

NGK Spark Plugs (UK) Ltd, 7-8-9, Garrick Industrial Centre, Hendon, London, NW9 6AQ. Tel: 0181 202 2151/4.
Top quality sparking plugs.

Palmer Snell, 65 Cheap Street, Sherborne, Dorset, DT9 3BA. Tel: 01935 812218
Specialists in classic motorcycle auctions.

The Vintage Motor Cycle Club Ltd., Allen House, Wetmore Street, Burton-on-Trent, Staffordshire, DE14 1TR. Tel: 01283 540557
A classic motorcycle club with more than 12,000 members, world wide, that caters for the interests of those who own machines more than 25 years old.

APPENDIX 4 - SERVICE HISTORY

This Chapter will help you keep track of all the servicing carried out on your classic motorcycle and may even save you money! A classic motorcycle with a service history is always worth more than one without. Although this book's main purpose is to give invaluable advice to anyone carrying out their own servicing, you can make full use of this section even if you have a dealer or a mechanic carry out the work for you. It will enable you to specify the jobs you want to have carried out on your motorcycle and, once again, it will ensure you to keep that all-important service history. Even if your motorcycle doesn't have a history that goes right back to when it was new, keeping this Appendix complete will add to your machine's value when you come to sell it. Obviously it won't be enough just to tick the boxes; keep all your receipts when you buy oil, sparking plugs and other consumables or parts. That way you will also be able to return any faulty parts if needs be.

IMPORTANT NOTE! The Service Jobs listed here are intended as a check list as well as keeping a record of your motorcycle's service history. It is most important that you refer to *Chapter 3, Service Intervals, Step-by-Step* for full details of how to carry out each job listed here and for essential SAFETY information, all of which you must be aware before you carry out the work.

Before carrying out a service on your motorcycle, you will need to purchase all the right parts. Please refer to *Chapter 2, Buying Spares,* for information on how to buy the right parts at the right prices and where to find your machine's frame and engine numbers for correct identification purposes. This will help make sure you buy the correct parts first time.

Wherever possible, the Jobs listed in this section have been placed in a logical order or grouped together, so that you will not have to move from one area to another in random fashion. Not only will this save you time but it should also help ensure all the Jobs are completed on an area by area basis.

You will also find a space after each service interval in which to write down the date, price, and seller's name every time you buy consumables or accessories. Once again, do remember to keep the receipts! There is also space for you to date and sign the Service Record or for the dealer's stamp to be applied.

As you progress through the Service Intervals, you will notice that the work carried out at, say, *Every 500 Miles or Every Month, whichever comes first,* is repeated at each one of the following Service Intervals. The same applies to the *Every 3,000 Miles or Every Six Months* interval. Much of it is also repeated at *Every 6,000 Miles or Every Twelve Months.* Every time a Job or a set of Jobs is repeated from an earlier Interval, we show this as a reminder in the form of a tinted area on the page. You can then see more clearly which Jobs are unique to the level of service your machine has reached.

You may be surpised to find all the major Service Intervals, right up to *Every 18,000 Miles or Every Three Years* contain Jobs that are unique to that Service Interval. That's why we have continued the Service History right up to the Three Years Interval.

EVERY 500 MILES, MONTHLY, OR BEFORE LONG JOURNEYS, WHICHEVER COMES FIRST

This list is shown, complete, only once. Otherwise it would have been necessary to repeat the same items 35 more times over the 3-year period! They are, however, included with every longer Service from *Every 3,000 miles/Three months* on, as a reminder that each of the monthly Jobs should be carried out as part of every Service.

Job 1.

☐ Check engine oil level.

Job 2.

☐ Check clutch lever free play.

☐ Adjust clutch

Job 3.

☐ Remove battery.

☐ Check electrolyte level.

☐ Check vent pipe (if fitted).

Job 4.

WATER COOLED ENGINES ONLY

☐ Top-up coolant.

Job 5.

☐ Adjust primary chain tension.

☐ Adjust final drive chain tension.

☐ Adjust wheel alignment.

☐ Adjust side-car alignment.

☐ Lubricate final drive chain in situ.

Job 6.

☐ Check tyre pressures.

Job 7.

☐ Adjust front drum brake.

☐ Adjust rear drum brake.

☐ Check stop light operation.

Job 8.

☐ Check headlamp and pilot lamp.

Job 9.

☐ Check rear lights.

Job 10.

MORE MODERN MACHINES ONLY

☐ Check indicator lights.

Job 11.

☐ Grease steering head bearings.

☐ Re-pack wheel hubs.

☐ Grease speedometer drive gearbox.

☐ Grease rear suspension.

Job 12.

☐ Clean bike thoroughly.

EVERY 1,500 MILES - OR EVERY THREE MONTHS, WHICHEVER COMES FIRST

These jobs are similar to the *Every 500 Miles* jobs but don't need to be carried out quite so regularly. Once again, these jobs are not shown with a separate listing for each *1,500 Miles/Three Months* interval but they are included as part of every *3,000 Miles/Six Month Service* list and for every longer Service Interval. Preferably commencing with Job 12, so that you start off with a clean bike.

Job 2.

☐ Check clutch lever free play.

☐ Adjust clutch

Job 3.

☐ Remove battery.

☐ Check electrolyte level.

☐ Check vent pipe (if fitted).

Job 4.

WATER COOLED ENGINES ONLY

☐ Top-up coolant.

Job 5.

☐ Adjust primary chain tension.

☐ Adjust final drive chain tension.

☐ Adjust wheel alignment.

☐ Adjust side-car alignment.

☐ Lubricate final drive chain in situ.

Job 6.

☐ Check tyre pressures.

Job 7.

☐ Adjust front drum brake.

☐ Adjust rear drum brake.

☐ Check stop light operation.

Job 8.
☐ Check headlamp and pilot lamp.

Job 9.
☐ Check rear lights.

Job 10.
MORE MODERN MACHINES ONLY

☐ Check indicator lights.

Job 11.
☐ Grease steering head bearings.

☐ Re-pack wheel hubs.

☐ Grease speedometer drive gearbox.

☐ Grease rear suspension.

Job 12.
☐ Clean bike thoroughly.

Job 13.
FOUR-STROKE ENGINES ONLY

OPTIONAL

☐ Change engine oil.

Job 14.
☐ Check tyre condition and tread depth.

☐ Check security bolt, when fitted.

Job 15.
☐ Adjust sparking plug gap.

Job 16.
☐ Check HT lead/s.

MULTI-CYLINDER ENGINES ONLY

☐ Check distributor.

Job 17.
☐ Check contact breaker gap.

☐ Overhaul contact breaker.

☐ Check magneto drive chain tension.

☐ Lubricate magneto drive chain.

EVERY 3,000 MILES - OR EVERY SIX MONTHS, WHICHEVER COMES FIRST

All the Service Jobs in the tinted area have been carried forward from earlier service intervals and are to be repeated at this service. Preferably commence with Job 12, to start with a clean bike.

Job 2.
☐ Check clutch lever free play.

☐ Adjust clutch

Job 3.
☐ Remove battery.

☐ Check electrolyte level.

☐ Check vent pipe (if fitted).

Job 4.
WATER COOLED ENGINES ONLY

☐ Top-up coolant.

Job 5.
☐ Adjust primary chain tension.

☐ Adjust final drive chain tension.

☐ Adjust wheel alignment.

☐ Adjust side-car alignment.

☐ Lubricate final drive chain in situ.

Job 6.
☐ Check tyre pressures.

Job 7.
☐ Adjust front drum brake.

☐ Adjust rear drum brake.

☐ Check stop light operation.

Job 8.
☐ Check headlamp and pilot lamp.

Job 9.
☐ Check rear lights.

Job 10.
MORE MODERN MACHINES ONLY

☐ Check indicator lights.

Job 11.
☐ Grease steering head bearings.

☐ Re-pack wheel hubs.

☐ Grease speedometer drive gearbox.

☐ Grease rear suspension.

Job 12.
☐ Clean bike thoroughly.

Job 13.
FOUR-STROKE ENGINES ONLY

OPTIONAL

☐ Change engine oil.

Job 14.
☐ Check tyre condition and tread depth.

☐ Check security bolt, when fitted.

Job 15.
☐ Adjust sparking plug gap.

Job 16.

☐ Check HT lead/s.

MULTI-CYLINDER ENGINES ONLY

☐ Check distributor.

Job 17.

☐ Check contact breaker gap.

☐ Overhaul contact breaker.

☐ Check magneto drive chain tension.

☐ Lubricate magneto drive chain.

Job 18.

☐ Change engine oil.

☐ Clean metal gauze filter.

☐ Replace oil filter (when fitted).

☐ Clean mesh filter in oil supply pipe (when fitted).

Job 19.

☐ Lubricate DC dynamo.

☐ Check/adjust dynamo drive.

Job 20.

OPTIONAL

☐ Adjust carburettor/s.

TWIN CARBURETTOR MODELS ONLY

☐ Synchronise carburettors.

Job 21.

☐ Check/change air filter.

Job 22.

☐ Change primary chaincase oil.

Job 23.

☐ Final drive chain lubrication.

☐ Final drive chain alteration/repair.

Job 24.

☐ Check and lubricate cables and rods.

Job 25.

☐ Check handlebar-mounted controls.

Job 26.

☐ Check wheels.

EVERY 6,000 MILES - OR EVERY TWELVE MONTHS, WHICHEVER COMES FIRST

All the Service Jobs in the tinted area have been carried forward from earlier service intervals and are to be repeated at this service. Preferably commence with Job 12, to start work with a clean bike.

Job 2.

☐ Check clutch lever free play.

☐ Adjust clutch

Job 3.

☐ Remove battery.

☐ Check electrolyte level.

☐ Check vent pipe (if fitted).

Job 4.

WATER COOLED ENGINES ONLY

☐ Top-up coolant.

Job 5.

☐ Adjust primary chain tension.

☐ Adjust final drive chain tension.

☐ Adjust wheel alignment.

☐ Adjust side-car alignment.

☐ Lubricate final drive chain in situ.

Job 6.

☐ Check tyre pressures.

Job 7.

☐ Adjust front drum brake.

☐ Adjust rear drum brake.

☐ Check stop light operation.

Job 8.

☐ Check headlamp and pilot lamp.

Job 9.

☐ Check rear lights.

Job 10.

MORE MODERN MACHINES ONLY

☐ Check indicator lights.

Job 11.

☐ Grease steering head bearings.

☐ Re-pack wheel hubs.

☐ Grease speedometer drive gearbox.

☐ Grease rear suspension.

Job 12.

☐ Clean bike thoroughly.

Job 13.

FOUR-STROKE ENGINES ONLY

OPTIONAL

☐ Change engine oil.

Job 14.

☐ Check tyre condition and tread depth.

☐ Check security bolt, when fitted.

Job 15.

☐ Adjust sparking plug gap.

Job 16.
☐ Check HT lead/s.

MULTI-CYLINDER ENGINES ONLY
☐ Check distributor.

Job 17.
☐ Check contact breaker gap.
☐ Overhaul contact breaker.
☐ Check magneto drive chain tension.
☐ Lubricate magneto drive chain.

Job 18.
☐ Change engine oil.
☐ Clean metal gauze filter.
☐ Replace oil filter (when fitted).
☐ Clean mesh filter in oil supply pipe (when fitted).

Job 19.
☐ Lubricate DC dynamo.
☐ Check/adjust dynamo drive.

Job 20.
OPTIONAL
☐ Adjust carburettor/s.

TWIN CARBURETTOR MODELS ONLY
☐ Synchronise carburettors.

Job 21.
☐ Check/change air filter.

Job 22.
☐ Change primary chaincase oil.

Job 23.
☐ Final drive chain lubrication.
☐ Final drive chain alteration/repair.

Job 24.
☐ Check and lubricate cables and rods.

Job 25.
☐ Check handlebar-mounted controls.

Job 26.
☐ Check wheels.

Job 27.
DRUM BRAKES ONLY
☐ Remove and check brake shoes.
☐ Lubricate brake operating cam.
☐ Replace brake shoes.

DISC BRAKES ONLY
☐ Check pads.
☐ Replace pads.

Job 28.
☐ Check seating.

Job 29.
☐ Check instruments.

Job 30.
TWO-STROKE ENGINES ONLY
☐ Clean exhaust system.

ALL TYPES
☐ Check for tightness.

Job 31.
☐ Change gearbox oil.

Job 32.
☐ Change front fork oil.

Job 33.
☐ Check valve clearances.

Job 34.
☐ Renew spark plug/s.

EVERY 9,000 MILES - OR EVERY 18 MONTHS, WHICHEVER COMES FIRST

All the Service Jobs in the tinted area have been carried forward from earlier service intervals and are to be repeated at this service. Preferably with Job 12, to start work with a clean bike.

Job 2.
☐ Check clutch lever free play.
☐ Adjust clutch

Job 3.
☐ Remove battery.
☐ Check electrolyte level.
☐ Check vent pipe (if fitted).

Job 4.
WATER COOLED ENGINES ONLY
☐ Top-up coolant.

Job 5.
☐ Adjust primary chain tension.
☐ Adjust final drive chain tension.
☐ Adjust wheel alignment.
☐ Adjust side-car alignment.
☐ Lubricate final drive chain in situ.

Job 6.
☐ Check tyre pressures.

SERVICE HISTORY

SERVICE HISTORY

Job 7.
- ☐ Adjust front drum brake.
- ☐ Adjust rear drum brake.
- ☐ Check stop light operation.

Job 8.
- ☐ Check headlamp and pilot lamp.

Job 9.
- ☐ Check rear lights.

Job 10.
MORE MODERN MACHINES ONLY
- ☐ Check indicator lights.

Job 11.
- ☐ Grease steering head bearings.
- ☐ Re-pack wheel hubs.
- ☐ Grease speedometer drive gearbox.
- ☐ Grease rear suspension.

Job 12.
- ☐ Clean bike thoroughly.

Job 13.
FOUR-STROKE ENGINES ONLY
OPTIONAL
- ☐ Change engine oil.

Job 14.
- ☐ Check tyre condition and tread depth.
- ☐ Check security bolt, when fitted.

Job 15.
- ☐ Adjust sparking plug gap.

Job 16.
- ☐ Check HT lead/s.

MULTI-CYLINDER ENGINES ONLY
- ☐ Check distributor.

Job 17.
- ☐ Check contact breaker gap.
- ☐ Overhaul contact breaker.
- ☐ Check magneto drive chain tension.
- ☐ Lubricate magneto drive chain.

Job 18.
- ☐ Change engine oil.
- ☐ Clean metal gauze filter.
- ☐ Replace oil filter (when fitted).
- ☐ Clean mesh filter in oil supply pipe (when fitted).

Job 19.
- ☐ Lubricate DC dynamo.
- ☐ Check/adjust dynamo drive.

Job 20.
OPTIONAL
- ☐ Adjust carburettor/s.

TWIN CARBURETTOR MODELS ONLY
- ☐ Synchronise carburettors.

Job 21.
- ☐ Check/change air filter.

Job 22.
- ☐ Change primary chaincase oil.

Job 23.
- ☐ Final drive chain lubrication.
- ☐ Final drive chain alteration/repair.

Job 24.
- ☐ Check and lubricate cables and rods.

Job 25.
- ☐ Check handlebar-mounted controls.

Job 26.
- ☐ Check wheels.

EVERY 12,000 MILES - OR EVERY TWENTY FOUR MONTHS, WHICHEVER COMES FIRST

All the Service Jobs in the tinted area have been carried forward from earlier service intervals and are to be repeated at this service. Preferably commence with Job 12, to start with a clean bike.

Job 2.
- ☐ Check clutch lever free play.
- ☐ Adjust clutch

Job 3.
- ☐ Remove battery.
- ☐ Check electrolyte level.
- ☐ Check vent pipe (if fitted).

Job 4.
WATER COOLED ENGINES ONLY
- ☐ Top-up coolant.

Job 5.
- ☐ Adjust primary chain tension.
- ☐ Adjust final drive chain tension.
- ☐ Adjust wheel alignment.
- ☐ Adjust side-car alignment.
- ☐ Lubricate final drive chain in situ.

Job 6.

☐ Check tyre pressures.

Job 7.

☐ Adjust front drum brake.

☐ Adjust rear drum brake.

☐ Check stop light operation.

Job 8.

☐ Check headlamp and pilot lamp.

Job 9.

☐ Check rear lights.

Job 10.

MORE MODERN MACHINES ONLY

☐ Check indicator lights.

Job 11.

☐ Grease steering head bearings.

☐ Re-pack wheel hubs.

☐ Grease speedometer drive gearbox.

☐ Grease rear suspension.

Job 12.

☐ Clean bike thoroughly.

Job 13.

FOUR-STROKE ENGINES ONLY

OPTIONAL

☐ Change engine oil.

Job 14.

☐ Check tyre condition and tread depth.

☐ Check security bolt, when fitted.

Job 15.

☐ Adjust sparking plug gap.

Job 16.

☐ Check HT lead/s.

MULTI-CYLINDER ENGINES ONLY

☐ Check distributor.

Job 17.

☐ Check contact breaker gap.

☐ Overhaul contact breaker.

☐ Check magneto drive chain tension.

☐ Lubricate magneto drive chain.

Job 18.

☐ Change engine oil.

☐ Clean metal gauze filter.

☐ Replace oil filter (when fitted).

☐ Clean mesh filter in oil supply pipe (when fitted).

Job 19.

☐ Lubricate DC dynamo.

☐ Check/adjust dynamo drive.

Job 20.

OPTIONAL

☐ Adjust carburettor/s.

TWIN CARBURETTOR MODELS ONLY

☐ Synchronise carburettors.

Job 21.

☐ Check/change air filter.

Job 22.

☐ Change primary chaincase oil.

Job 23.

☐ Final drive chain lubrication.

☐ Final drive chain alteration/repair.

Job 24.

☐ Check and lubricate cables and rods.

Job 25.

☐ Check handlebar-mounted controls.

Job 26.

☐ Check wheels.

Job 27.

DRUM BRAKES ONLY

☐ Remove and check brake shoes.

☐ Lubricate brake operating cam.

☐ Replace brake shoes.

DISC BRAKES ONLY

☐ Check pads.

☐ Replace pads.

Job 28.

☐ Check seating.

Job 29.

☐ Check instruments.

Job 30.

TWO-STROKE ENGINES ONLY

☐ Clean exhaust system.

ALL TYPES

☐ Check for tightness.

Job 31.

☐ Change gearbox oil.

Job 32.
☐ Change front fork oil.

Job 33.
☐ Check valve clearances.

Job 34.
☐ Renew spark plug/s.

Job 35.
☐ Renew contact breaker points.

Job 36.
☐ Grease wheel bearings.

Job 37.
☐ General tightness check.

Job 38.
☐ Clean battery terminals.

Job 39.
☐ Check steering damper.

Job 40.
DISC BRAKES ONLY

SPECIALIST SERVICE

☐ Check/overhaul disc brake callipers.

EVERY 15,000 MILES - OR EVERY THREE YEARS, WHICHEVER COMES FIRST

All the Service Jobs at this service interval have been carried forward from earlier service intervals and are to be repeated at this service. Prefereably commence with Job 12, to start with a clean bike.

Job 2.
☐ Check clutch lever free play.
☐ Adjust clutch

Job 3.
☐ Remove battery.
☐ Check electrolyte level.
☐ Check vent pipe (if fitted).

Job 4.
WATER COOLED ENGINES ONLY
☐ Top-up coolant.

Job 5.
☐ Adjust primary chain tension.
☐ Adjust final drive chain tension.
☐ Adjust wheel alignment.
☐ Adjust side-car alignment.
☐ Lubricate final drive chain in situ.

Job 6.
☐ Check tyre pressures.

Job 7.
☐ Adjust front drum brake.
☐ Adjust rear drum brake.
☐ Check stop light operation.

Job 8.
☐ Check headlamp and pilot lamp.

Job 9.
☐ Check rear lights.

Job 10.
MORE MODERN MACHINES ONLY
☐ Check indicator lights.

Job 11.
☐ Grease steering head bearings.
☐ Re-pack wheel hubs.
☐ Grease speedometer drive gearbox.
☐ Grease rear suspension.

Job 12.
☐ Clean bike thoroughly.

Job 13.
FOUR-STROKE ENGINES ONLY
OPTIONAL
☐ Change engine oil.

Job 14.
☐ Check tyre condition and tread depth.
☐ Check security bolt, when fitted.

Job 15.
☐ Adjust sparking plug gap.

Job 16.

☐ Check HT lead/s.

MULTI-CYLINDER ENGINES ONLY

☐ Check distributor.

Job 17.

☐ Check contact breaker gap.

☐ Overhaul contact breaker.

☐ Check magneto drive chain tension.

☐ Lubricate magneto drive chain.

Job 18.

☐ Change engine oil.

☐ Clean metal gauze filter.

☐ Replace oil filter (when fitted).

☐ Clean mesh filter in oil supply pipe (when fitted).

Job 19.

☐ Lubricate DC dynamo.

☐ Check/adjust dynamo drive.

Job 20.

OPTIONAL

☐ Adjust carburettor/s.

TWIN CARBURETTOR MODELS ONLY

☐ Synchronise carburettors.

Job 21.

☐ Check/change air filter.

Job 22.

☐ Change primary chaincase oil.

Job 23.

☐ Final drive chain lubrication.

☐ Final drive chain alteration/repair.

Job 24.

☐ Check and lubricate cables and rods.

Job 25.

☐ Check handlebar-mounted controls.

Job 26.

☐ Check wheels.

18,000 MILES - OR EVERY THREE YEARS, WHICHEVER COMES FIRST

All the Service Jobs in the tinted area have been carried forward from earlier service intervals and are to be repeated at this service. Prefereably commence with Job 12, to start with a clean bike.

Job 2.

☐ Check clutch lever free play.

☐ Adjust clutch

Job 3.

☐ Remove battery.

☐ Check electrolyte level.

☐ Check vent pipe (if fitted).

Job 4.

WATER COOLED ENGINES ONLY

☐ Top-up coolant.

Job 5.

☐ Adjust primary chain tension.

☐ Adjust final drive chain tension.

☐ Adjust wheel alignment.

☐ Adjust side-car alignment.

☐ Lubricate final drive chain in situ.

Job 6.

☐ Check tyre pressures.

Job 7.

☐ Adjust front drum brake.

☐ Adjust rear drum brake.

☐ Check stop light operation.

Job 8.

☐ Check headlamp and pilot lamp.

Job 9.

☐ Check rear lights.

Job 10.

MORE MODERN MACHINES ONLY

☐ Check indicator lights.

Job 11.

☐ Grease steering head bearings.

☐ Re-pack wheel hubs.

☐ Grease speedometer drive gearbox.

☐ Grease rear suspension.

Job 12.

☐ Clean bike thoroughly.

Job 13.

FOUR-STROKE ENGINES ONLY

OPTIONAL

☐ Change engine oil.

Job 14.

☐ Check tyre condition and tread depth.

☐ Check security bolt, when fitted.

Job 15.
☐ Adjust sparking plug gap.

Job 16.
☐ Check HT lead/s.

MULTI-CYLINDER ENGINES ONLY
☐ Check distributor.

Job 17.
☐ Check contact breaker gap.
☐ Overhaul contact breaker.
☐ Check magneto drive chain tension.
☐ Lubricate magneto drive chain.

Job 18.
☐ Change engine oil.
☐ Clean metal gauze filter.
☐ Replace oil filter (when fitted).
☐ Clean mesh filter in oil supply pipe (when fitted).

Job 19.
☐ Lubricate DC dynamo.
☐ Check/adjust dynamo drive.

Job 20.
OPTIONAL
☐ Adjust carburettor/s.

TWIN CARBURETTOR MODELS ONLY
☐ Synchronise carburettors.

Job 21.
☐ Check/change air filter.

Job 22.
☐ Change primary chaincase oil.

Job 23.
☐ Final drive chain lubrication.
☐ Final drive chain alteration/repair.

Job 24.
☐ Check and lubricate cables and rods.

Job 25.
☐ Check handlebar-mounted controls.

Job 26.
☐ Check wheels.

Job 27.
DRUM BRAKES ONLY
☐ Remove and check brake shoes.
☐ Lubricate brake operating cam.
☐ Replace brake shoes.
DISC BRAKES ONLY
☐ Check pads.
☐ Replace pads.

Job 28.
☐ Check seating.

Job 29.
☐ Check instruments.

Job 30.
TWO-STROKE ENGINES ONLY
☐ Clean exhaust system.
ALL TYPES
☐ Check for tightness.

Job 31.
☐ Change gearbox oil.

Job 32.
☐ Change front fork oil.

Job 33.
☐ Check valve clearances.

Job 37.
☐ General tightness check.

Job 41.
☐ Check electrical wiring.
☐ Check switch gear.

Job 42.
☐ Check crankcase breather pipes.

Job 43.
☐ Compression test.

Job 44.
DISC BRAKES ONLY
☐ Renew hydraulic brake fluid.

Job 45.
☐ Clean and check carburettor/s.

Job 46.
☐ Check petrol tap.